My Father, the Messiah

My Father, the Messiah

A MEMOIR

Gil Z. Hochberg

Duke University Press
Durham and London 2026

© 2026 DUKE UNIVERSITY PRESS. All rights reserved
Project Editor: Lisa Lawley
Designed by Courtney Leigh Richardson
Typeset in Garamond Premier Pro by Copperline Book Services

Library of Congress Cataloging-in-Publication Data
Names: Hochberg, Gil Z., [date] author
Title: My father, the Messiah : a memoir / Gil Z. Hochberg.
Description: Durham : Duke University Press, 2026. | Includes bibliographical references and index.
Identifiers: LCCN 2025020318 (print)
LCCN 2025020319 (ebook)
ISBN 9781478032915 paperback
ISBN 9781478029434 hardcover
ISBN 9781478061649 ebook
Subjects: LCSH: Hochberg, Gil Z., 1969– | Middle East specialists—United States—Biography | College teachers—United States—Biography | Fathers and daughters—Correspondence | People with bipolar disorder—Family relationships | Mental illness—Religious aspects | Israel—Politics and government—1993– | LCGFT: Autobiographies
Classification: LCC DS61.7.H63 A2 2026 (print) | LCC DS61.7.H63 (ebook) | DDC 956.9405092 [B]—dc23/eng/20250903
LC record available at https://lccn.loc.gov/2025020318
LC ebook record available at https://lccn.loc.gov/2025020319

Cover art: The author and her father, Chapel Hill, North Carolina, 1972. Photograph: Courtesy of the author. Background: Adobe Stock/Nadi.

My father's face. Dark complexion, long sideburns, meaty lips. When my father smiles, his whole face lights up. His deep brown eyes shine and his mouth opens wide. Over the years, as he got older and sicker, his face became puffy and his skin flaky and pale. He lost his smile and his eyes turned vacant.

———————

My father had two faces. The lively gleeful face of his youth and the drained face of the second part of his life. The former shined and glittered; the latter I'd rather forget but cannot.

Contents

Prologue   1

2013   East Jerusalem
Bus Station   3

2013   Tel Aviv
Modern Death   5
Sepsis   7

1991   Geha & Petach Tikvah
The Ward   8
Lithium   11

2016 Los Angeles
Lithium, His Words   12

1992 Tel Aviv
King Messiah   14

1989 Tel Aviv
Coming Out   16

1987 Tel Aviv
Second Marriage   18

1989–1995 Tel Aviv
Madness   20
Rabin's Letter   22
On Snails and Blue Dye   23
Madness on a National Scale   25

2013 Tel Aviv
Burial   27
Shivah   28
His Study   32
The Tomb   33
Drifting   34
Out of Place   35
Wall in Hebron   36
His Will   38

2013–2015 Los Angeles
Mourning and Melancholia   39

2016 | 1976–1985 | 1970–1975
Los Angeles · Ann Arbor & Bloomington · Chapel Hill
Letters   42
Summers   45
Underwater   47
Hasidic Hits   48
Free to Be … You and Me   49
Walk like a Girl!   52
Queer Survival   55

2016–2017 Los Angeles
Not All Playful   59
Remembering to Forget   61
Papa Gorilla   61
First Attempt   63

2018 | 1980–1986 New York
Bleecker Street   64
I Am My Father's Archivist   67
My Parents   68

1972–1976 Chapel Hill
Time Makes a Story Out of Pain   73
I Am the Guard   77
Family Albums, 1968–1974   77
Jesus   79

2020–2022 New York

Visiting the Archive at the Time of Pandemic	84
Reading, Writing; Past, Present	88
Lost and Found in the Archive	89
My Father's Penis	93
Uninvited Memories	95
Summer on a Boat	98
Writing Memory	101
The Hochberg Toes	103
Break	106
My Father, the Messiah	108
My Father, the Statistician	110

JANUARY 2023 New York

Beyond Interpretation	117
National Amnesia, Forced Forgetting	119
Tsipe and Hirschel Hochberg	123

JANUARY 2018 Tel Aviv

Kazakhstani Lover	127

APRIL 2023 Petach Tikvah

The Cousins	132
Le-Yossi!	142

MAY 2023 | 1949–1963 New York ·
Israeli Army Prison, Yahud
A Jewish Jean Genet   144
Yeshiva Boy by Day, Gangster by Night   148

2023–2024 New York
Messianic Jargon, or Lessons of a Madman   150
My Queerness, Divine Intervention   153
Miracles   154
Diet Poem   157
Shit Matters   159

2024 New York
My Siddur   164
His Voice, Mine   166
Let Me Out!   167

AUGUST 2024 Rebordões
Impossible Ending   169

Acknowledgments   177
Notes   181
Bibliography   185

Prologue

I have become my father's archivist. He has become the object of my writing. At times. But writing about him is also writing with him. This book is written between our bodies. Between identities, temporalities, memories, spaces, genders, and sexualities. Between the living and the dead. It is made of his writings and mine: his writings to me, his writings about writing, his writing about my writings, and my writings about his writing. Not mine. Nor his. He/I. His/Mine. We. Us. He. I. My memory, his. His body, mine?

Writing from this blurred space is an attempt to shake off the fixity of common narratives of loss, grief, mourning, and recovery. This book follows no arc of healing. It is an attempt to render the space of writing, as well as that of memory, mourning, and archiving, as a queer space. Which, as such, is just as messy at the end as in the beginning.

This is also a very Jewish text in the sense that it resists a linear perception of time and the idea of progress. "Judaism doesn't know the difference of time; what was then is now," I learned from my father. And, as Walter Benjamin reminds us, with the prohibition against "investigating the future," Jews are obliged to remember rather than think forward. And yet, as both Benjamin and my father knew well, this doesn't mean that the future is devoid of magic, because at any given moment the "Messiah might enter."[1]

Playing with Dad. Chapel Hill, North Carolina, 1972.

2013

East Jerusalem

Bus Station

I was at the central bus station in East Jerusalem around noon, queuing for a minibus heading to Ramallah, when my father's wife called. Miriam never called me. We weren't close; we barely tolerated each other. So when I saw her name on the phone, I knew something must have happened. Still, I was just about to get on the minibus, and my sabbatical from UCLA was about to end, and I was running out of time, and I still had a lot of research to do, and I had a meeting to attend. I needed to get on that bus.

It was extremely hot for late April. It felt like mid-August. I was burning in my white, long-sleeved, button-down shirt that I wore so I'd look professional when I met the professor I'd been trying to get ahold of for months. Jerusalem's dry air felt like an open oven. It hurt to inhale.

I have to get on this bus, I told myself. But the phone kept ringing. I knew I had to pick up. My mind was racing. *I can't miss this ride. I can't give up my place in the line. I've been standing here under this beating sun for almost an hour already. Why is she calling me?!*

Damn it. The ringing stopped and started right back. I had no choice. I picked up. "Gilly," Miriam's metallic voice was shaky, "Abba be-beit cholim, be-tipul nimrats" (Dad is in the hospital, in the ICU).

"Gilly, are you there? Do you hear me?" Miriam's voice was so alarmed. I froze.

"You need to come now!"

I can't stand her voice, I thought, a second before I snapped back into reality.

"Ken, okay, ken," I responded nervously, at once aware of the fact that I was speaking Hebrew in the middle of a long line of Palestinian passengers in East Jerusalem. Self-aware and uncomfortable, I told Miriam, "I can't hear you well. I'll call right back."

I left the line and moved through the crowd, looking for a quiet place and some shade. My heart was racing, a combination of the heat and the news I'd just received. I found a naked tree that gave an illusion of shade behind the central area, where all the minibuses were parked, and called Miriam. "I'm in Jerusalem. What happened?"

"Leave!" she shouted. "Come to Ichilov, now!" Her authoritative tone shocked me. I've never heard it before. *Ichilov* . . .

"Dad is in the hospital" were words I was used to hearing from her. But I would mostly hear them from afar. I'd been living in California for over twenty years, so visiting Ichilov, Tel Aviv's central hospital, was not an option. This time I was around. Close enough. Still, I was in East Jerusalem where I was spending my sabbatical, doing research for a book about the visual politics of the Israeli occupation. While only an hour drive away from Tel Aviv, these two cities are worlds apart. The transition required serious mental preparation. So, when Miriam said, "Come now!" I initially got confused. It didn't seem possible. It took me a couple more minutes to realize that I had no choice. I had to move into action.

I put the phone in my backpack and then looked around at the busy streets and the minibuses. I knew I had to make my way from East Jerusalem to the west side of the city, but I suddenly lost my sense of direction. Partly it was the heat, but mostly it was the dread that filled me each time I had to navigate between the two divisions of this torn-apart and artificially glued-together city infested with police and armed border control. The schism between the transition from Arabic to Hebrew and from a reality marked by visible military occupation to a reality thriving in its concealment was the topic of my book in progress. Still, it was much easier to write about it than to move through it.[2]

Robotically I got into a taxi, making my way out of the crowded bus station in the East to the central bus station in the West. Within fifteen minutes, my physical reality changed radically. Once at the new station, I got into a large, new, air-conditioned bus with velvety blue seats. Quite different from the small, old, overheated, and overcrowded minibuses that took Palestinian passengers from East Jerusalem into the West Bank. I was tired. I felt something akin to nothing. A nothingness that filled my chest with a very unpleasant feeling. The seat next to me was empty, so I placed my backpack on it and closed my eyes. An hour later I woke up in Tel Aviv.

2013

Tel Aviv

Modern Death

My father wasn't a healthy man. By sixty, he'd already had two heart attacks and several strokes. He suffered from internal bleeding caused by years of overdosing on steroids, chronic back pain, colitis, high blood pressure, and an irregular heartbeat. This in addition to his bipolar disorder and the psychotic episodes that led to living through three suicide attempts. Hospitals were not foreign to him, or to me. I hated visiting him in my early twenties. When he wasn't in urgent care, he was in psychiatric wards. Now, fatigued, I made my way to the fourth floor of Ichilov—Internal Med, Urgent Care. I had visited him here before. I knew the routine: wash hands; put on facial mask, gown, latex gloves; sign in; and enter the quarantine room. I also knew what to expect. I knew I'd find him puffy, unconscious, and immobile, connected to machines that kept him alive. I knew I would find Miriam sitting by his side, holding his hand, her eyes distraught.

The ICU is a place of waiting. There is not much to do there but wait. Waiting to see on what side the patient who is between life and death would end. For the next two weeks, this was what Miriam and I did. We waited. We took turns. Sometimes sitting in his room, sometimes in the visitors' waiting area. Waiting has its own pace, its own temporality. Two weeks of waiting in the hospital can feel like a year, even two. But sometimes it can also feel like a single day. Waiting stretches and shrinks linear time, making it irrelevant. Along the way, it devours everything else. Time stops. Thinking stops. Feelings stop. Waiting.

Sitting by my dad's bed meant following the perfectly rhythmed movement of his chest, up and down, as if dancing to the sounds of the ventilator. I spent most of the time looking at his half-naked, hairy chest, which was now shaved in patches. An entire network of tubes crossed it, passing liquids in and out of his pasty body. I was afraid to touch him at first, but I eventually placed my hand on his swollen, cold fingers. *Dead or alive?* A person kept alive by a machine is somewhere in between.

For the past two decades, my dad had looked, walked, and smelled much older than his biological age. Still, for years, even decades, each time he got sick, each time he was hospitalized, he somehow recovered. His illnesses and self-inflicted injuries left his body scarred and his soul deflated. Yet, he lingered. He just kept going—falling and getting back up on his feet again, like a cat. *Is he going to wake up this time?* As the days passed, with him remaining unconscious and connected to the ventilator, I realized his chances were growing slimmer. Still, I was expecting him to bounce back. Like he always did.

Two weeks passed. I arrived in the morning to replace Miriam, who had spent the whole night at the hospital. I found her seated by my father, her eyes red from crying, holding his hand. "It's freezing in here," I said, not knowing what else to say. Miriam lifted her eyes, looked at me, and said nothing. We were both tired, anxious, drained. The two of us were going through this painful experience together, but our togetherness didn't bring us closer. We were never close, and now, being in this small room with my father unable to witness us, we didn't even feel the need to pretend or act out the false intimacy we used to perform for him. We simply accepted the silence between us, like we accepted the unreasonably cold temperature in the room.

Shortly after, a nurse came in and asked us to sit in the waiting area during the doctor's visit. Later I came to suspect her words weren't true and that he was already dead before we exited the room. I don't know for sure, but I suspect it is true because just before, instead of hearing the familiar mechanical sound of the ventilating machine pumping air into his lungs, we heard a strange hollow rattle. Both Miriam and I noticed it. Whether he died then or later, I don't know, but I will never forget that horrid rattle. For me it remains the sound of his departure; his lungs evacuating the machine.

Within no more than an hour of waiting, the nurse called us back to the room and told us he passed away. Miriam collapsed in her seat and began to wail. I approached the door and looked on as two nurses pulled out all the tubes from his body—one for urine, one for shit, one providing oxygen, one pumping blood, one a feeding tube. Then they turned off the monitors. The background buzzing and clicks of the machines were silent now. It was dreadfully quiet. The nurse encouraged Miriam to go out, saying, "We'll soon have to take the body. My condolences."

His dead body, swollen and full of blue marks from all the tubes that ran through it for the last two weeks, lay flat between Miriam and me as we stood there, looking down at the bed, in silence. We avoided each other's eyes. Wife and daughter, we'd perfected this avoidance over the decades, and now we drifted away effortlessly, each to her own sorrow.

I took a last long look at my father's body. Remembering how, just a few weeks ago, I had visited him at his apartment and we both laughed about how much we loved ice cream and how we "live for sweets." Looking at him now, half naked, lifeless, I missed his smile. I even missed the comforting sounds of the ventilator that kept his chest rising and falling until those last moments. A perfect rhythm. I never thought I would miss it.

The next day, I would see his body again, at the graveyard. Someone had to identify the body before burial. Miriam refused, so it was me. In a small back room, a rabbi exposed his face from under the tallit prayer garment. Only thirty-six hours had passed but he had already become a thing. Gray like a stone. Unrecognizable.

The only comfort I could find at that moment was in knowing that he didn't have to witness his prosaic death. He wouldn't have liked it at all. He tried to do much better in the few times he attempted suicide: cutting his neck and almost bleeding to death, cutting his wrists in a hot bath, climbing over the window ledge and attempting to jump from the sixth floor. Yes, he would have liked a spectacular death with lasting, gory images. I imagine he would have wanted us to see his body shattered into pieces and covered with blood. Instead, he got to die in a small freezing hospital room, connected to tubes, looking drained, washed up, and covered with a white sheet. A prosaic, tragic, modern death.

He would have found it utterly humiliating.

Sepsis

"Are you Professor Hochberg's daughter?" A young, slim, tired-looking doctor approached me.

"Yes," I answered, thinking this question sounded strange. Being a literature professor, I was used to being called "Professor Hochberg" but never "Professor Hochberg's daughter."

"Can you follow me, please?" the doctor asked me. "I've printed the death report."

I walked behind him into a small room, the size of a closet, where he handed me an envelope and said, "I am very sorry." Then, muttering, "Sepsis."

"Sepsis?" I looked back at him.

"Sepsis, yes. The cause of death." He said this in a monotonous and measured tone and added, as if he was doing me a great favor by extending the conversation, "Complete shock. System collapses. Sepsis. The details are in here." He pointed at the envelope, turned around, and left.

I walked out of the hospital in the heat and found a nearby shady bench. I sat down to read the report. The list of preconditions was long: hyposmolality, symptomatic hypernatremia, Addison's disease, colitis, ischemic heart disease, depression, bipolar disorder, ulcerative colitis, drug-induced osteoporosis, type 2 diabetes, Barrett's esophagus, renal failure. But the death summary was brief: "Patient, 67, arrived in the ER confused and incoherent.... Twenty-four hours later his kidneys began to fail rapidly and he deteriorated neurologically in a similarly fast manner.... After five days he was declared septic. He continued to deteriorate in the ICU. Cause of death: Sepsis."

"Sepsis." I still didn't understand what this word meant. The doctor explained it was "a systemic infection," but I wanted to know more about the mysterious, almost tantalizing word: "sepsis." When I got back home, the first thing I did was look it up. I learned it came from Greek. "Sepsis: The decomposition of animal or vegetable organic matter."[3] With this in mind, I finally grasped what happened to my father. His death was not sudden after all. On the contrary, he was dying for a very long time. His sick, scarred, overmedicated, rotten body was decomposing slowly over the past two decades. "Sepsis" was the cause of death. But in truth, my father was sepsis-ing for years. I just refused to see it.

1991

Geha & Petach Tikvah

The Ward

"He's alive" was the first thing Miriam told me when I met her at Geha, a psychiatric hospital not far from Tel Aviv. Two hours beforehand, his younger brother Haim called me and told me in a matter-of-fact voice, "Gilly, Yossi cut himself. Miriam found him. She saved him. But he lost a lot of blood."

Haim always called my dad "Yossi." Most people did, even though his name was Yosef. My grandmother used to call him "Yosale," and I mostly called him "abba," but when I wanted to be sweet I called him "*abbale*." Now my *abbale* had slashed his throat and I had no way to understand this. I was twenty-one. He was forty-five. We were both too young to deal with death. He survived. He ended up spending almost five months in a closed unit in Geha, which soon became my own *Gehinnom* (hell).

The drive to Geha was familiar to me because it was on the way to Petach Tikvah, where my grandparents—his parents, Tsipe and Hirschel—lived for most of my childhood. I'd always noticed the ugly cement building on the right. I didn't know it was a psychiatric ward, but it symbolized for me the end of Tel Aviv and the beginning of the no-man's-land, which included ghostly, hopeless cities like Petach Tikvah.

The literal Hebrew meaning of *Petach Tikvah* is "the opening of hope." The irony of this never escaped anyone. I thought about it every time I visited my grandparents' dark, depressing apartment. Petach Tikvah offered no hope. It was and remains a remarkably unattractive outskirt. No wonder the cement building was a psychiatric hospital. What better than a ward to announce the beginning of the end of hope?

I hated visiting Geha. First the parking lot, then the walk of shame through the corridors, then the smelly elevator, and finally the white metal door with the small, circular window where a nurse would appear long after I rang the buzzer. Third floor, 5A. "A closed unit for high-risk patients." Once I buzzed, I waited. From behind the door, I heard patients screaming, nurses yelling, and steps. Lots of steps. Eventually the door would open and a nurse—usually a male nurse, usually Palestinian, the ones employed in the high-risk units—would let me in. *Poof*, the intense smell would assail me. A shocking, rotten smell: a mixture of urine, sweat, and unwashed bodies. Reminiscent of the notorious European asylums from the nineteenth century that I read about.

Inside, the space was divided into rooms, about four patients per room, and a large communal area that faced the nurses' bay. Some patients, those no longer forcefully tied down, roamed around. Unshaven, dirty, some barefoot. Visitors tended to lower their eyes in shame or simply to avoid the pressure of engagement. I hated the forced exchanges ("How is your father doing?") and I hated having to be nice to the doctors, who were always impatient. But above all, I hated being in his room, sitting by his bed. For the long months he was there, he was always in the exact same position: curled around himself like a fetus. Immobile, his face to the wall, his skin dry, his eyes shut, his mouth half open and attached to a feeding tube, his face unshaven, his fingernails too long, his feet swollen. *A dead shrimp*. It was horrible to see him like this and even worse to feel disgusted at the sight. Soon enough, my repulsion was replaced by guilt.

After three months of zero success with medications, the psychiatrist decided to try electroshock treatments. They'd lift him from the bed like dragging a heavy corpse and place him into a wheelchair. He looked dead on his way there and even deader on his way back. I could still see the red scar and the fresh stitches on his neck, dried blood around them. I felt sorry for him, but mostly I felt scared, realizing I had likely lost him. That was the first time I felt that way, but it wasn't the last. I kept losing him over and over again for the following twenty years. It never got easier.

Toward the end of his stay in the high-risk unit, he made some progress. His psychiatrist, Dr. Chermesh, a man in his late forties, told Miriam and me that the electroshock therapy had worked: "Yossi is ready to move to unit 5B, a closed unit with less restriction." In the new unit, he shared a room with three other patients. "Here we don't need to tie the patients down," a nurse tells us. "It is much more relaxed." My father didn't seem to notice the change. He was still lying in bed, his face to the wall, curled up like an embryo. If there was progress, only Dr. Chermesh and his team could see it.

Although 5B wasn't as loud as 5A, with less screaming and no resistant patients being forcibly tied down, it wasn't less of a hell. It still reeked of urine and, because patients were allowed to walk around, there were more interactions between visitors and patients—something I found particularly hard. While my father continued to be unresponsive, neighboring patients took every opportunity to engage. There was a short, bald man with the rough voice of a heavy smoker who grew attached to Miriam and followed her around, calling her "mommy." There was a young man across from my dad who paced around me, asking me to help plan his escape. And finally, there was a skinny, bearded man who had a guttural laugh and a constant heavy cough. Whenever I sat down by my father's bed, he would stand close by and stare at us. Sometimes he would taunt, laugh, and cough, but usually he would leave after a short while.

One day, he stood right next to us and began to yell, pointing at my dad, "Wake up, Professor Hochberg, wake up!" He shouted and then laughed hysterically, throwing his body back and forth. "Wake up! Professor Hochberg is not waking up! He is *sssssssssleeeeeeeping* all day! Baby, baby! Wake up!" I looked around, hoping to catch sight of a nurse, but no one came. His voice got louder and louder, "Wake up, Professor Hochberg! Wake up N-O-W!!!" Then, before I had time to understand what was about to happen, he pulled down his hospital pants and pissed on my father's back, screaming and laughing hysterically. "Shoooooower time for Professor Hochberg sleepy baby, hahaha."

At first, I was paralyzed, mortified. Eventually I ran out of the room looking for help. A nurse got up slowly and followed me, hissing and cursing. He ordered me to wait outside, from where I could see him lifting my dad into a wheelchair. "Going to wash him," he muttered. The coughing man stayed in the room, and I could hear him laughing and roaring, "Professor Hochberg woke up! He woke up!"

Later that evening, they moved my father to another room. "I hear your father is an important professor," the same nurse told me the next day. "Don't worry, from now on, he is *my* patient. I'll keep an eye on Professor Hochberg."

By the time my dad was released from Geha, he had a diagnosis. Dr. Chermesh called Miriam and me to tell us my dad was "bipolar with acute psychotic episodes." He also told us that most likely he had been ill for many years, if not decades. "It wasn't until recently that mental patients got diagnosed, unless they found themselves in an extreme situation." Then he went on to reassure us that "as long as Yossi stays on the medications and continues to see me, he should be fine." And just before we left his office, he added, "Most importantly, make sure he continues to take the lithium."

Lithium

Like many people diagnosed with bipolar disorder and hypermania, my dad depended on lithium to regulate his extreme mood swings. And like most patients, he resented it. He was, to quote Dr. Chermesh, "one of those patients who refused to help themselves." This crude evaluation, of course, failed to acknowledge the many side effects of lithium as the reason behind many patients' resistance: cognitive dullness, brain fog, tremors, excessive thirst, weight gain, muscle ache, fatigue, decreased creativity, decreased libido.

How or why lithium works is a mystery. What is known, however, is that it does. People have written odes to lithium, memoirs about lithium, even as the medical world remains in the dark about the precise mechanism of its impact on the brain. "Oh cerebellum, oh Lithium, do your job," Shira Erlichman sent out her plea in *Odes to Lithium*.[4] "[Lithium is] this kind of amazing miracle salt. It also is a metal. It's present everywhere on Earth, in the galaxy, in our bodies, for everyone," Jaime Lowe comments in an interview about her memoir, *Mental*.⁵

A miracle salt indeed. As long as my father took it, he was stabilized. He was even able to return to work: teaching, doing research, delivering talks. The problem was that "no pill can help deal with the problem of not wanting to take pills," to borrow Kay Redfield Jamison's words describing her own resistance to lithium in *An Unquiet Mind*.⁶ Like most people with bipolar disorder, my father depended on lithium to maintain his sanity, but knowing this made him resist it all the more.

From 1991 forward, the cycle was always the same: He would fall into depression and then begin to take lithium, often overdosing in the hope of speeding up his recovery. Then, as soon as he got better, within three or four months, he would forget all about the depression and begin to cut down or just do away with the medication.

"I can't think with it.

"I hate how swollen it makes me.

"It makes me feel numb!

"It makes me dumb!

"I have no ideas!"

Lithium kept him stable, which also meant it took away his fire and kept his mania at bay. And boy, my dad *loved* his mania, more than all the rest of us hated it.

2016

Los Angeles

Lithium, His Words

Three years had passed since my dad died. I'd been carrying a folder full of his writings with me as we moved from one house to another in Los Angeles. Among the hundreds of papers, I found a short text titled "Lithium: My Nemesis" (Lithium: *Oyevee*) dated November 1992. It is written in Hebrew in black pen with some words underlined, traces of his shaky handwriting leaving little lines across the words covering the yellowish paper. I was surprised to see that he wrote about his complex relationship with the mineral. Even more so, I was shocked to discover that he had his own explanation for resisting it, and it had little to do with reduced focus, libido, or creativity. Instead, it was all about a mighty war between Judaism and Christianity:

> My first encounter with lithium was in 1991. I was hospitalized and diagnosed with manic-depressive disorder. Well that is how *they* called it. The doctors. They decided I was sick and they gave me this drug. But from the very beginning I had a bad feeling about it. The psychiatrist, Dr. Chermesh, insisted that I must continue to take it. I did for a few months, but eventually I stopped. I realized that he (like all doctors) shares the same primitive attitude toward "my mania." They think it needs to be contained like a "monkey in the zoo." But I know better! I know that I am naturally filled with joy (they call my joy "mania") because God gave it to me. I know I am gifted and creative above average, because God made me his vessel. And I also know that when I am depressed it is because God wants me to be. The doctors tell me that without this mineral, I will become sick. But I don't fear illness anymore. My ups and downs are simply the way God is testing my strength. So, I have no intention of ever taking lithium again. I know things the psychiatrists don't know. They don't believe in Him. But I see now how my whole life has been leading me toward this point and this divine mission: God sent me here to fight them! Psychiatrists, like all other doctors, are Christian idol-worshippers. God sent me to save the Jewish people from this modern Christian medical fiction. It is my role as the real Messiah to put an end to this. *Kol Yisrael yesh lahem chelek* [All of Israel has a part in the next world]. This idiom means that Jews must no longer be or see doctors. Modern medicine is anti-Jewish! Only Christians believe in such nonsense. *Am Yisrael* must return to practice our authentic Jewish ways and beliefs. As the Torah says (Exodus 15:26!): *Ani Adonai Rof'ekha* [I, God, your healer] Listening to doctors is a sin. From now on: Only God. I say no lithium! No to psychiatry! God alone is my medicine!!!

My father had a theological reasoning and explanation for his mental illness and even for his resistance to treating it with medicine. Taking lithium, in his mind, would be a Christian thing to do. Listening to his psychiatrist would be a betrayal of Jewish principles. Within the Jewish cosmology he believed in, there could be no other doctor but God.

Once a scientist himself, a biostatistician at that, who had worked closely with pharmaceutical companies, my father came to denounce all science as Christian and the modern belief in "man" as anti-Jewish. In rejecting lithium, he rejected his old self and adopted what in his mind was his newly authentic self. Once a scientist, he was now the Messiah. And, truly, who would expect the Messiah to be taking lithium?

1992

Tel Aviv

King Messiah

My dad's manic episodes were much easier for me to stomach than his prolonged depressive interludes. I was young and didn't realize that each period of hypermania was bound to be followed by yet another fall into the dark abyss. The cycle was tragic and seemingly unavoidable. But it took a few more acute depressive episodes and two more suicide attempts for me to realize that. Perhaps I was naive, or, more likely, I really wanted to believe, each time anew, that my father was "finally healed." So every time he got energized, returned to work, and seemed well functioning, I, like Miriam, overlooked the warning signs of his fast approaching, frantic euphoria. I was happy that he was happy.

Not long after he was released from Geha, his mood improved. First slowly, then rapidly. The times I'd come to visit him and Miriam, I'd find him talkative and jubilant. He talked about miracles, the signs he received from God, and about running as a candidate for the position of the Messiah. It seemed a bit off, clearly, but I saw no harm in it. I found it quite entertaining overall and enjoyed listening to his upbeat declarations. He was "blessed," he "found his calling," he "was chosen," he was about "to save his people." Sometimes he would order Miriam to join him in a celebratory dance. Stamping their feet, my dad twirling her around, they sang *"Am Yisrael Chai!"* (Long live the people of Israel). I watched them like one watches a stand-up comedy show, entertained with the jokes but slightly uncomfortable with the self-deprecation that is almost always part of the humor.

The times he broke into lengthy lectures about God's bond with his people, the Promised Land, and the building of the Third Temple I enjoyed less. But I couldn't stop him. He was unstoppable. So, I just listened, pretending to believe him.

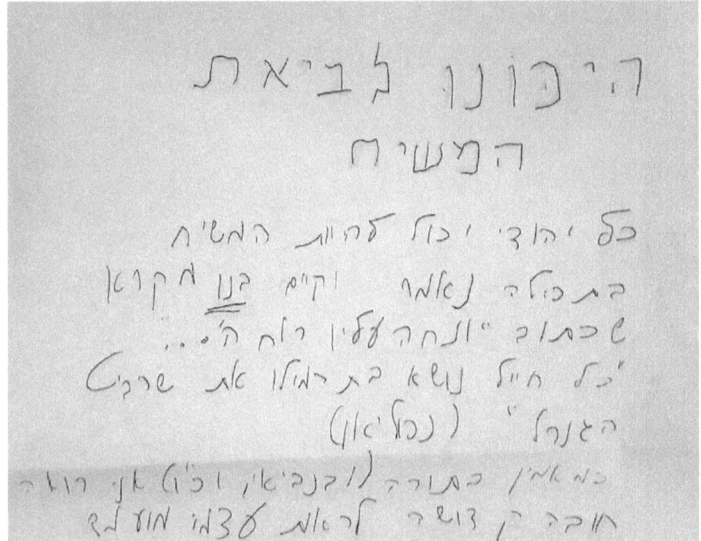

"Prepare for the Arrival of the Messiah." One of my dad's handwritten pamphlets, 1992.

"The true king Messiah will arise and reestablish the monarchy of David as it was in former times!" My father welcomed me to his living room and asked me to join Miriam on the sofa. He informed us, talking about himself in the third person, that "Professor Yossef Hochberg has just been chosen as *Mashiach Emet* [real Messiah]. . . . Anyone who does not believe in him or one who does not anticipate his coming denies not only the prophets but also the Torah and Moses, our teacher!" With these words by Maimonides (Rambam), he ordered us to stay quiet. "You are my first followers!" He announced, "You both have been chosen."[7]

His conviction was alarming, but I intentionally pushed away my concerns. I told myself there was no reason to overreact. After all, this wasn't the first time he had entertained feelings of grandeur, and over the years I learned not to take his self-congratulatory declarations too seriously. This was a man who told me when I was a kid that he could "see through walls," that he was "the best scientist to have ever existed," that he was "about to change the world," that he could "lift a building with his nose." So now that he announced himself as the Messiah, I wasn't totally surprised. *Let the man be happy*, I assured myself; and if his happiness meant he needed to believe all of this, so be it.

Without lithium, it took very little for my dad to reach the highs of manic euphoria. Even a few days without meds would result in radical mood shifts, and he'd be conversing with the prophets and turning his statistics classes into lectures on the mathematical proof of God's existence. Any attempt to pull him out of that elation resulted in screaming bouts and violence. Miriam feared him, and Haim and I eventually gave up on trying to intervene.

1989
Tel Aviv

Coming Out

I had just turned twenty when my dad told me for the first time that he was the Messiah. The two of us were in a coffee shop near Tel Aviv University for a meeting set up by my mother, his divorcée of fourteen years. She called us both a couple of days earlier and ordered us to meet to discuss what she described as "an emergency situation." She never talked to him, which gave this event an aura of exceptionality, and for my dad this meant we were dealing with something of great urgency indeed. Something worth *her* calling *him*. He could hardly hide his excitement when he called me and said, "Let's make it easy and meet at our usual place."

"Our usual place" was a simple coffee shop walking distance from campus. It served nothing but coffee, tea, and dry pastry. But the truth was that "*our* usual" was not so usual at all. We hardly met in those days, and when we did, it was rarely around campus and hardly ever just the two of us. This despite the fact that I was a first-year philosophy major on the same campus where he had taught for several years now: Tel Aviv University. A grassy campus, not too large, where the walk from the humanities building to the math building, where his office was located, was no longer than seven minutes max.

Now, summoned to the café, we were both visibly nervous, shifting restlessly in our seats, sipping coffee, and pretending to enjoy the stale croissants. He was nervous because he had no idea why we were meeting; I was nervous because I did.

Just a few days earlier, I came out to my mom, hoping, assuming in fact, that being a poet, a bohemian, and an open-minded romantic soul, she would embrace my lesbianism, hesitant as it was. Far from it. She didn't welcome the news; worse, she denied it: "You are not!" was her first reaction. Her second, which followed right after, leaving me no time to respond before she left the room distraught, was: "We're *not* going to talk about this anymore. You'll talk to your father about it. These kinds of perversions run in his family!"

So there we were, father and daughter, once very close, now quite removed, meeting in a café to discuss "perversions." Being forced into this one-on-one meeting felt contrived. And given my mom's reaction, I wasn't anticipating an empathetic response from my dad. I had no idea what to expect. I no longer knew the man. Not since he returned to live in Israel, remarried, became religious, and started to speak in tongues about Moses, Abraham, and God's promise. I was hoping this was all a fleeting phase and had no idea it would be followed by decades of mental illness.

Finally, after a long silence, my dad looked at me, smiled, and said, "So, *yalda*, what's the emergency?" "*Yalda*," not "daughter," not "my child," but "girl-kid." That is what he always called me, using the Hebrew feminine for *kid*. *Yalda*. His soft voice brought back a wave of nostalgic memories.

When I was growing up, the two of us were very close, despite living on opposite sides of the North Atlantic. I lived with my mother and stepfather in a small suburb just outside of Tel Aviv while he, a roaming professor, lived in various university towns across the United States: Chicago, Berkeley, Ann Arbor, Bloomington, but mainly New York City. During the school year, our communication was based on letter exchange. International calls were too expensive back then, and email didn't exist. I still have his letters. Over one hundred of them, written and sent to me between 1976 and 1986. Sweet letters. He wrote them all in Hebrew, detailing his daily activities, sharing his plans for our next summer vacation, and often complaining about not getting enough letters back from me. During the school year, I waited for his letters. But more than anything, I waited for the summer.

I spent my summers with him. Far from Israel, far from my mother and her migraines, far from the chores of daily life, far from school. Summers were my dream time. Filled with pleasure and the stuff of vacation: amusement parks, cartoons, bubblegum, pools, water parks, ice cream, fried chicken, and plenty of cereal filled with sugar, preservatives, and artificial flavors. Everything a young child growing up in Israel in the 1970s could only dream of or, at best, see on her black-and-white TV.

"*Yalda*," his voice woke me up from my daydreaming. I felt a twisting in my chest. I missed him. I missed us and our special bond. It was gone now, the magic of our summers. Like my childhood. I looked at him, this man in his mid-forties. I used to know him so well, or so I thought. His eyes looked sad when I looked back up at his face.

I don't want to hurt him, I thought. Then, *I don't want to be hurt by him*.

"Come on, what is it, Gilly? Drugs? Are you pregnant? You want to quit college?"

"No. No," I responded, a bit disappointed with the list of clichés he'd pulled out of his pocket. I took a deep breath and spewed it out: "I think I'm a lesbian. Maybe bisexual."

My dad lowered his eyes, took another sip of his coffee, then released a soft smile and said, "That's it? This is the emergency?! The big news?" He seemed overtly disappointed. Then he pulled his chair even closer to mine, locked eyes with me, and said in a prophetic tone, "None of this is important, Gilly: gay, straight, bisexual. Whatever. None of this matters. These are all *inyanai dyuma*." He used the rabbinic Aramaic term *inyanai dyuma* (matters of the daily), which took me by surprise and surely elevated the conversation to a register far beyond daily matters.

Then, before I had a chance to respond, he continued, "These are just small details in God's grand plan ... Silly insignificant details. Don't waste your time on *ha-olam ha-zeh* [this world]. The only thing that matters is *ha-olam ha-ba* [the world to come]."

I stared at him, hoping to detect a smile, but no. He was dead serious. And after another sip of what was left of his coffee, he lifted his arms up high and pronounced theatrically, "Thank you for sharing your news. Now let me tell you mine." He leaned over even closer, and whispered in my ear: "Ani Ha-mashi'ach ... Aba shelakh nivchar ... Abba shelkh massi'ach emet" (I am the Messiah ... Your father was chosen ... I am the real Messiah). And with a triumphant smile he added, "Now *that* is big news!"

1987

Tel Aviv

Second Marriage

In 1987, after spending thirteen years in the United States, my dad moved back to Israel and joined the math department at Tel Aviv University as a professor of statistics. One would think this would bring us closer, now that we were living in the same country for the first time in over a decade. But instead, this was the beginning of the end of our fierce attachment. The magic of our shared summers was no more. I was no longer a dreamy child, and he was no longer a lonely bachelor. A year after he returned, he met Miriam, and soon after they got married. But that was only the beginning of the tragedy that was about to unfold.

Slowly but surely, my dad began to embrace his religious upbringing, but in a very different fashion than the one I was familiar with as a child. Up until this point, he shared with me the joy of Hasidic singing and dancing. I loved it. But something else was brewing now. Something I initially didn't recognize as terrifying, because I didn't recognize it at all. My father was becoming a zealous, fundamentalist Zionist who suddenly spoke in a language totally foreign to me about *ha-am ha-nivchar* (the chosen people), *admat ha-kodesh* (the holy land), and "our enemies": *Amalek*, the Arabs, the goyim. I didn't think much of it at first. Mostly because I was young and his new life with Miriam was not the focus of my attention. I removed myself.

Miriam seemed kind and I wanted to like her. She was pretty and elegant. Her hair was long and reddish-brown, her skin was olive-toned and smooth, and she dressed nicely in flowery summer skirts. But the overt power dynamic of their rapport made it hard for me to be around them from early on. His megalomaniacal need for constant adoration was met by her equally strong drive to survive. She was an abused woman, freshly divorced, with three older children, and she needed him for financial stability and status. He was a lonely man who finally found a woman who stuck around. Their relationship was based on a codependency that grew monstrous over time.

I know what you're thinking: "jealous daughter." There was that too, undeniably. After all, he and I were very close up until these two got together. But it was really the insular and creepy nature of the world they built together that was the cause of my antagonism. Just months into their marriage, they established a routine based on all kinds of rituals, known to the two of them alone. He would say something, and she would repeat it verbatim; he would begin to hum, and she would stop whatever she was doing at the moment, stand by his side, and join in the singing. Hasidic songs. Always Hasidic songs. Some in Hebrew, mostly in Yiddish, the mother tongue of them both.

And as the bond between them grew, the rest of his relationships faded away; not only with me but with his colleagues, his few friends, his brother, and even his mother, to whom he had been so attached until then. He no longer met me every week for lunch, as we did for the first year after he moved to Israel. His colleagues stopped visiting, and his daily calls to my grandmother ended. She even complained about it to me. We all lost him.

Miriam and my dad's codependency tied them to each other and blocked the rest of us out. He needed her to boost his ego, and she needed him to need her. Soon enough, they drifted into a world inhabited by the two of them alone, with him, as we all came to realize, becoming the Messiah and her becoming his only faithful follower.

1989–1995
Tel Aviv

Madness

In the months that followed our mutual "coming out" meeting at the café, my dad was in an elevated mood. He told me about the many miracles he'd experienced and the signs he'd received from God. I decided to enjoy it. Little did I know how fast this feverish joy would turn into agonizing despair. But before he came crashing down from the high, things got higher.

Madness. Any other word would take away from the spectacle of his performances over the months building up to his collapse in 1991. Mathematical equations scrawled on torn pages hung all over their apartment, ecstatic dances, demonstrations of various *otot u-moftim otot u-moftim* (signs and wonders), all of which he received from God, "just like Moses!"

"A bottle of water was empty when I left the room but then filled on its own"; "the lights were turned off, and then a deep voice spoke through the walls and said, 'Let there be light,' and all the lights turned on"; "Miriam was not home, but when I whispered her name, she suddenly appeared right before me." These marvels and miracles went on for several long months, close to a year. He felt "creative like never before," "joyful like never before," "energetic like never before." He "found the mathematical proof for God's existence, and soon the entire world would see that God is one and he, Yosef Hochberg, is His one and only true loyal servant."

Eventually, things began to take a bad turn. First came paranoia. He started to accuse neighbors and colleagues of trying to sabotage his messianic mission. Then he declared there was a spy in the math department at Tel Aviv University responsible for "leaking state secrets to the enemy." He accused Miriam of thinking he was a false messiah and made her prove her loyalty by performing various rituals: burning things, swearing allegiance, dancing around him. Worried about him, or afraid of his reactions, she did. His speech grew faster and louder. Miriam mentioned that he was sleeping less and spending more and more time talking to King David, Elisha, and other biblical friends. "It's all in the scriptures! All in the scriptures!" he yelled each time Miriam or I asked him to calm down.

Finally, depression settled in and worsened. Day by day, he was becoming lifeless. And the dynamic between Miriam and him changed accordingly. As long as he was euphorically manic, she was his devoted subject. Now that depression kicked in, he became helpless, and she was his only trusted caregiver. It was as if those two were playing master and slave, changing positions, dancing to the drums of my father's mood swings. I was shut out. Everyone was.

I knew it wasn't easy to live with my father, and I appreciated Miriam for taking care of him. I also knew she feared him, because his brother Haim told me that my dad would hit her whenever she challenged his words. I felt sorry for her, I really did. She was fragile and used to abuse. But it was hard to witness their dynamic. I never felt she did anything out of malice, only out of her own insecurity.

Over the years, with his mental illness joined by other medical problems, Miriam had become not only his wife but his nurse, his only friend, his cook, his mother, and ultimately his savior. When he cut his wrists and throat, bleeding into a hot bath, she found him almost lifeless and saved him. When he tried to jump out of the window of their sixth-floor apartment, she was able to stop him by calling the police. When he overdosed, she rushed him to the hospital. Each time he almost died, she was there to save him and bring him back to life. And, sadly, the more dependent he was, the more secure she became.

With time, the manic episodes got more extreme. As did the depression. Beginning in 1991, my dad was in and out of the psychiatric hospital. In 1993, he claimed that Jehovah ordered him "to jump from the sixth floor of his apartment building to join Moses at the Ohel Moed [Tent of Meeting]." In 1995, he received secret messages about the secretary of the math department: "She was a dangerous spy." He locked her in a bathroom for several hours. Luckily, she decided not to file a complaint. On another occasion he was "called to a secret meeting with the prophet Elisha." He was about to set his study on fire when

Miriam smelled smoke and stopped him. What began as performances of happy Hasidic dances with his wife in the living room grew steadily into monstrous shows of roaring, throwing things, cursing, and, more than once, harming himself: "God told me to prove my dedication!"

If only I was tuned in enough, mature enough, wise enough to see this coming. By the time I did, it was already too late. Perhaps it was always already too late.

Rabin's Letter

From 1989 to 1991, my dad sent out dozens of letters to famous rabbis and politicians in Israel, declaring his status as the (one and only) true Messiah. He validated his status by arguing that he came from a famous rabbinic bloodline, with direct ties to the Radziner rebbe, Grand Rabbi Gershon Chanoch Henech Leiner of Radzyn, also known as Ba'al ha-tekhelet (Master of Blue).[8] And not only did he have such a distinguished rabbinic lineage, he was also both "Gadol ba-torah" (versed in Jewish matters) and a scientist. As such, he was "perfectly set to deliver God's message in different registers to different audiences: be-leshon chakhamim le-me-lumaday torah, ve-belshon chol le-me-lumaday mada" (in a sacred language to students of the Torah and in secular language to students of science).

In letter after letter, he offered his help and desperately sought recognition from famous rabbis and politicians. Few, if any, answered his letters, but he remained convinced that his time would come. One day he received a letter from the office of Prime Minister Yitzhak Rabin to whom he'd written to "not give Jewish land to the enemy." He was euphoric. The letter, likely written by an office worker, simply read:

Dear Professor Hochberg,

Prime Minister Rabin wishes to thank you for your letter and commend you for being a responsible and involved citizen.

My father was elated. He interpreted this formal response as a secret message. "Look! Look at the date of the letter: 'April 9.' That means 04/09 = 49!" he exclaimed to Miriam and me. We tried to follow. He continued, "Forty-nine times the Torah mentions the color *tekhelet*, the blue dye on the corners of the tzitzit! You see?! I'm the great-great-great-great-grandson of the rabbi named for this color, Ba'al ha-tekhelet. Make the connection! Forty-nine times—*tekhelet*—and Rabin's letter sent on 4/9. It all makes sense. It's divine intervention!"[9]

He taped the letter to the wall in his study alongside all the other notes and cuttings he considered to be signs of one coherent reality.

"God is one, redemption is coming, and Yosef Hochberg is the true Messiah."

On Snails and Blue Dye

From 1987 onward, through the rest of his life, my dad was obsessed with the question of the special blue dye that marked tzitzit. When I say "obsessed," I mean this was the only thing he was willing to talk about and with great passion. Any attempt to change the topic of conversation would result in him getting upset and eventually shutting down.

At the entrance to his apartment, my dad hung a sign he had handwritten with a thick black marker. One couldn't come in without immediately seeing it:

> Speak to the Children of Israel and say to them that they shall make themselves tzitzit [fringes] . . . and they shall place upon the tzitzit of each corner, a thread of *tekhelet*!

He copied this verse from Numbers (Ba-midbar), the fourth book of the Torah, and made sure I read it out loud each time I visited. I presumed he did the same for other visitors, although there were fewer and fewer of those as time passed by.

"You should be very proud to learn that I belong to the great Hasidic lineage of Rabbi Gershon Henoch Leiner of Radzin, Ba'al ha-tekhelet!" my father announced soon after I entered his apartment. This announcement followed other details. He spewed them out manically. I didn't even try to stop him. "You must know! The *tekhelet* is mentioned in the Torah forty-nine times! It is the most important thing about the tallit . . . not a small matter, no, no!"

"The Rambam said that only one-half of one tzitzit should be blue!"

"Rashi said it resembled the color of a pure evening sky!"[10]

"In the Talmud it is described as made of the blood of a *hilazon* [snail], a special sea snail."

My father's eyes sparkled and his voice shook. He could barely contain his excitement. "Did I tell you that Rabbi Leiner—*our blood!*—was the one who found the snail!"

Not the snail again, I thought to myself. I'd already heard this story at least ten times. But I didn't want to hurt his feelings or interrupt his joy. So I pretended I was interested.

My dad went on (per usual) to explain the family's relationship to this famous rabbi known as Ba'al ha-tekhelet: "My great-great-grandfather married Sipora, who was the sister of Hadas, who was the wife of the Rabbi Leiner!... So this means that my great-grandfather was the brother-in-law of Ba'al ha-tekhelet! We are the descendants of this important man!"

Initially, I thought my father was inventing these stories about snails and rabbis and a special blue used to dye the ends of the tallit. I assumed these stories were all part of his recently activated messianic reality and his madness. But with time I learned that this part—the craziest of all—was actually not made-up and not part of his hallucinations. This made the whole thing feel even crazier to me: The stuff about the blue dye, the snail, our family genealogy, and men from the nineteenth century traveling the shores of Italy looking for a sea snail was actually real.

At some point, my father's cousin Benny even showed me a conch the family had kept for decades. It was allegedly found by Rabbi Leiner and passed down from one generation to another. It turned out that my dad's snail stories weren't his alone. Many shared his obsessive preoccupation with the mysterious blue dye. A quick online search introduced me to a mad world indeed: Rabbis, biblical scholars, chemists, and oceanologists were all feverishly debating the exact specimen and searching the ocean for the alleged snail. I learned this was all part of a long tradition and an ongoing debate among various Hasidic groups. My dad's obsession, I realized, was part of a large-scale Jewish mania.

At some point, I even came across an announcement for an international conference in Jerusalem entitled "100 Years of *Tekhelet* Research." Participants included famous rabbis, academics, and politicians from all over the world. Everyone who was anyone was there. Everyone but my dad, despite dedicating so much time and energy into researching the blue dye.

You would think realizing my dad's snail obsession wasn't his alone would make me feel better. But no. It made it much more painful for me. Recognizing that this whole thing was "real" and was part of a lively conversation and community made me see my father less as mad and more as a tragic figure. He wasn't just a man who suffered from a delusional messianic complex; he had become, in my eyes, tragic in a much more profound way because he remained an outsider, even among those who shared his madness.

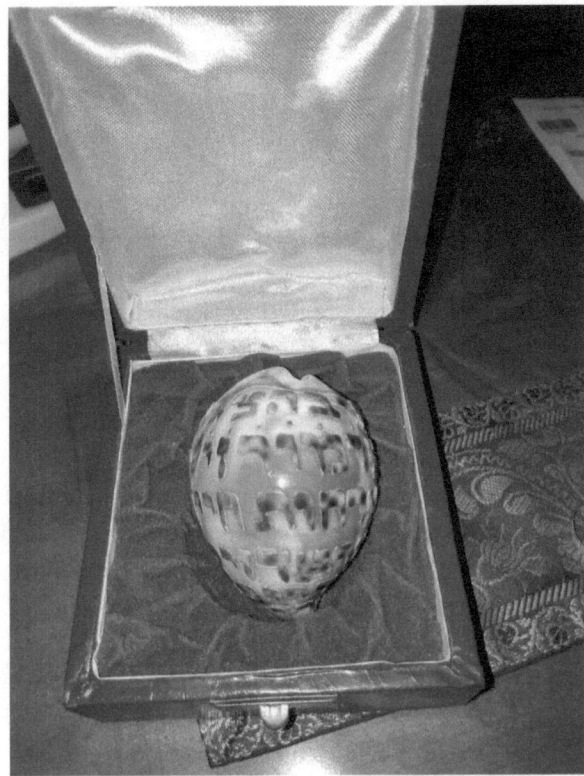

The conch allegedly found by Rabbi Leiner (Ba'al ha-tekhelet), kept and passed on for generations in our family.

Madness on a National Scale

In 1987, when my father began his research in the footsteps of his ancestor Rabbi Leiner to confirm the original source of the blue dye used for the fringes of the great priest of the first temple, he surely wasn't alone. He read about cuttlefish, squid, and snails, determined to prove that Leiner was right. He even made relentless attempts to enroll in the Izhbitza-Radzyn Yeshiva in the ultra-Orthodox city of Bnei Brak, only to be rejected flat out. He tried to visit the Center for the Dyeing of the Tekhelet established by the yeshiva but was denied access. He wrote to rabbis who never answered. He sent pictures of the alleged "original shell" found by Leiner. But the rabbis dismissed it as fake. He was heartbroken but didn't stop arguing that he alone, the Messiah, held the truth. "They are making a grave mistake," he told me and Miriam. "The original *tekhelet* is still hidden. Only I can find it."

Is he mad? I asked myself. *What makes a mad man?* What makes one man proclaiming to be the Messiah "mad" and another man with the same allegation a leader? A rabbi? A respected scholar with millions of followers? I never stopped asking myself this question.

Frankly, my father's manic rambling and preaching were no different from those uttered on Israeli TV and written in Israeli newspapers. He was part of a large and growing national movement, a messianic movement, an ethno-religious-messianic-national-Zionist movement. If he was mad (which I concluded he was), his madness reflected, and borrowed from, a collective psychosis. Still, one man proclaiming to be the Messiah ends up in a mental institution subjected to electroshock therapy. Another becomes a leader of the largest Hasidic movement in the world. Perhaps this is the true tragedy of madness.

One of the reasons it took time for us all to realize my father was gravely ill was that my dad wasn't the only one speaking feverishly about revelation, God, and the Messiah. Far from it. He was speaking the jargon of the time. Since the 1990s, the Promised Land, the anticipated revelation, and the arrival of the Messiah have become an ever-growing part of everyday public discourse in Israel, as the nation was becoming more overtly theocratic, messianic, and, some allege, even Christian.

In other words, my dad's madness was folded into the lingua franca of the time. He was regurgitating clichés and borrowed phrases he heard on TV, on the radio, on campus, and on the streets: "Eretz yisrael, le-am yisrael, lefi torat yisrael" (The land of Israel for the people of Israel by the Torah of Israel) or "Yeshuv ha-karka, kodem geola" (Settling in the land [of Israel] precedes redemption). His views were not particularly original. Everything he said was part of the growing zealous, religious, Zionist rhetoric that took over the country. If he was mad, so was the entire nation. A national psychosis that today, as I write in 2024, can no longer be denied by anyone.

2013

Tel Aviv

Burial

We buried my father the day after his death, as is the custom in Jewish law. "Do not linger with the dead." Miriam insisted he should be buried in the Orthodox section of the main cemetery in Tel Aviv. It happened to also be the hottest, ugliest, most barren part of the cemetery. We congregated under the vicious Israeli sun: Miriam, her thirty-year-old daughter, my father's brother Haim, his son Udi, a single colleague from the mathematics department at Tel Aviv University, and my father's four cousins.

A migraine was creeping down my neck, as it often does when I'm stressed. The sun was merciless, and I knew I'd better find some shade and water and cool myself off, but neither were to be found.

"You might as well be dead in this heat," I said to Udi, who replied with a tired smile, "Not for the faint of heart or the queers." Udi and I had a queer bond. I was ten years older than he, so when he first came out, I was his confidant. And together, we both speculated that our grandmother, Tsipe, who hated our grandfather, Hirschel, and was always bitter, must have been a closeted lesbian. "She was undoubtedly the genetic foundation for our shared Hochberg queerness," we humored ourselves. Now, under the beating sun, Udi was my only comfort and ally.

We were following Haim, two of my father's cousins, and the single colleague who together carried the body, tilting from side to side on the stretcher. A man from the Chevra Kadisha (Jewish burial society) gave the sign, and Haim and the others lifted up the stretcher and poured the body into the dirt hole. I heard it hit the ground. An ugly, muted sound. Then the four men, sweating in the heat, used shovels to dig and throw earth over the tallit-covered body. "Me'afar ba'ata ve-el a'far tashov" (From dust you came and to dust you shall return).

My temples were pulsing and a sharp pain flashed through my right eye. *I must find a way to get out of the sun. I have to close my eyes.* My thoughts were interrupted by the loud voice of the rabbi: "Eiifo ha-minyan?! Ma zeh, ein lakhem minyan?!" (Where is your minyan?! What is going on, you don't have a minyan?!). True, we didn't have the ten men required for the prayer of the Kaddish. The Chevra Kadisha man rushed over to nearby graves to solicit volunteers. Eventually we had ten penises, permissible to say the Kaddish:

> Yitgadal v'yitkadash sh'mei raba b'alma di-v'ra
> chirutei, v'yamlich malchutei b'chayeichon
> uvyomeichon uvchayei d'chol beit yisrael, ba'agala
> uvizman kariv, v'im'ru: "amen."

[Glorified and sanctified be God's great name throughout the world
which He has created according to His will.
May He establish His kingdom in your lifetime and during your days,
and within the life of the entire House of Israel, speedily and soon;
and say, "Amen."]

The pain in my right eye was killing me, sharp like a twisting knife. I hated Miriam for forcing us to stand in the unforgiving sun and subjecting us to this patriarchal ceremony. It was time for the women to approach the grave and place little rocks on the fresh mound of earth. As I bent down to grab a stone, the pain ran up from my eye, cutting through my skull. Then an aura: purple circles, larger and larger. I sat on the ground and held my head. "I have to vomit," I told Miriam.

"Not here!" she hissed at me.

I walked as far as I could from the grave. A cold sweat covered my body, then shivers began. I bent down to vomit. I wanted to get rid of it all: this migraine, the sun, the minyan, Miriam, the rabbi, Chevra Kadisha. But nothing came out.

Shivah

The shivah followed. I arrived, my head throbbing and my entire body depleted, at the modern building in Ramat Aviv C, a distinctly nouveau-riche suburb near Tel Aviv University. My father and Miriam had lived here in a large four-bedroom apartment since they got married in 1989. I grew up not far from here, in an older neighborhood, on the other side of the university.

The suburb as a whole is known as Ramat Aviv, but it is divided into distinct sections: A, B, C. By Israeli standards, Ramat Aviv comes close to the American suburban dream: grass and trees, quiet sidewalks, clean playgrounds, and even a boutique supermarket that carries outrageously priced Italian produce.

Ramat Aviv A was built in the late 1950s, with blocks of small, brownish apartment buildings. Ramat Aviv B has newer, taller buildings and larger apartments dating from the early 1960s. That's where I spent most of my childhood, in medium-high buildings with medium-sized apartments. Ramat Aviv C was built in the mid-1970s and expanded in the 1980s. It boasts the tallest buildings and the largest apartments. Only rich kids lived there. Growing up in this green, lethargic suburb, I learned to measure myself and everything else in threes: *low, middle, top, A, B, C.*

Walking to school, I had to cross Ramat Aviv A, and while visiting friends I sometimes ventured into C. These routine crossings never erased these unmarked borders and hierarchies; on the contrary, they highlighted them: *A, B, C, low, middle, top*. So when my father and Miriam bought an apartment in Ramat Aviv C, I couldn't help but feel elated, despite scrutinizing myself for the pettiness of my own feeling. They moved into the rich kids' neighborhood. And this meant that somehow, indirectly and a bit late, I too had finally arrived. I made it to the top.

Entering the elevator on the way to the shivah, I inhaled the familiar smell of lavender. Too thick and too sweet, it matched the tacky aesthetics of the lobby, crowded with mirrors and white marble. I made my way to the sixth floor. I had been here so many times before, but always to visit him. This time I knew he wouldn't be there.

The front door was already open and a death announcement, printed in thick, black Hebrew letters, welcomed me:

Prof Yosef Hochberg, Z"l,
Son of R. Zvi Z"l and Tsila Z"l, Halakh Le'olamo.
Avelim: Eeshto Miriam Hochberg, Bito Gil Hochberg, Achiv Haim Hochberg.

[Prof. Yosef Hochberg, of blessed memory,
Son of R. Tzi of blessed memory and Tsila of blessed memory, Deceased.
Mourning: his wife Miriam Hochberg, his daughter Gil Hochberg,
his brother Haim Hochberg]

I stepped in like a guest of honor: I was "the mourning daughter." The other honorary guests—the mourning brother and the mourning wife—were already there. The three of us, who otherwise rarely talked for the past decade, were now forced into a shared ceremonial mourning.

Others soon began to arrive: neighbors, relatives, a few of my father's colleagues. The living room was set up with plastic folding chairs. Those were set in the main area, between the dining room and the sofas, leaving the other half of the living room free to host the huge plants Miriam had collected over the years. The apartment was too small for this jungle, so the plants had to bend and grow horizontally once they reached the ceiling. Miriam always said they made the apartment "feel tropical." Under this tropical forest was my father's old brown

MY FATHER, THE MESSIAH 29

leather recliner. He sat in it for years, facing the TV. It was empty now, but I could still see the imprint of his heavy body on the leather and some coffee stains on one of the arms. Ten years he spent in this recliner under the jungle leaves. Looking at it empty now made his absence painfully visible. "That is Yossi's seat," Miriam announced repeatedly, each time a new guest came in. "Please don't sit in it."

My migraine was relentless and the growing cacophony of voices felt like a drill in my temples. Every relative, colleague, and neighbor in attendance shared memories and impressions:

"He was so charismatic."

"He was brilliant, simply brilliant."

"I remember Yossi as a child. He was so mischievous."

"Your dad was our leader."

"The first time I met Yossi, he told me he was going to change the way we do science."

"I didn't even know he was so sick."

The voices were bubbling, closing in on me as the room became more crowded. Did they really think I wanted to hear this? I was so tired and mentally drained. All I wanted was rest. I wanted to hug my children. I wanted to be alone. I wanted to take a warm bath. I wanted my grandmother, who was long dead, to sit and caress my hair. I wanted to eat warm oatmeal with butter. I wanted to be a little girl. I wanted to be a little girl with my dad at the pool. The last thing I wanted was to be there, surrounded by people I hardly knew.

People say the shivah is a brilliant Jewish invention. A way to support the mourners. The whole community comes together to hold the grief collectively and to make sure the mourners eat and drink and overcome the initial shock of loss. In theory, this is all true. But in reality, at least in *my* reality, the shivah was a nightmare. I was disoriented, achy, hungry, tired, and resentful for having to take part in endless small talk.

Days went by. Same small talk, same chatter, same lukewarm coffee. Miriam and I hardly exchanged a word. My kids, Omri (four) and Eli (seven), came once or twice with my partner, Keri. They didn't like being there, and I felt no need to subject them to the forced somber atmosphere or to Miriam's fake kindness. I spent my days there, from nine in the morning to nine in the evening, in the same black, torn T-shirt—as mourners, close relatives of the dead, are supposed to do—returning home to crawl into bed, deflated.

On the fourth day, or perhaps it was the fifth, surrounded by guests in chit chat, I began to imagine that the large plants were reaching out from the pots to grab and devour me and that my dad's recliner was breathing, expanding with every breath it took. I tried to move my eyes away from both recliner and plants. But as soon as I did, I got dizzy and nauseated. Everything in this apartment—the walls, the coffee table, the TV stand, the credenza—was overcrowded with memorabilia, porcelain figurines, postcards, decorative plates, and little flags. Small objects Miriam collected over the decades and displayed everywhere. Souvenirs from Niagara Falls, the Taj Mahal, the Czech Republic, the Kremlin, and even Auschwitz.

What is this compulsion of hers to collect and clutter? I asked myself, feeling increasingly irritable, squeezed between the huge plants and the tchotchkes with no escape. I looked up at Miriam, who was standing in the kitchen, and a terrifying thought crossed my mind: *This woman, who collected all these souvenirs, had turned my father into one of her memorabilia, tucked away under her plants.* I could see him sitting there in his recliner, as he had been doing for the past ten years. Sitting immobile, staring at the TV, waiting for her to come back from work. And she? She would always find him in the exact same place, just like the rest of her figurines.

I'd always had an uneasy relationship with Miriam, not only because her arrival in my father's life meant he became less available to me and the two of us grew distant but also because I never fully trusted her intentions. She was a strong woman who'd pulled herself out of a disastrous marriage with a violent gangster, raised three children on her own, and used her looks to her advantage. She was a survivor. And survivors tend to be dangerous, even when they have no bad intentions.

I knew she loved him. She took care of him, cooked for him, followed him around. Together they built their own insulated world made of Yiddish, religious ceremonies, and many trips around the world. All this until he got sick, very sick. She remained loyal to him, but like a survivor clinging to life, she did everything to keep him hers and hers alone. I trusted that she wanted to keep him happy. But she did so by looking away when he didn't take his pills, isolating him, and making him fully dependent on her.

Now, sitting squeezed between chattering guests, the huge plants and endless memorabilia closing in on me, I felt I had to flee it all, especially her. I got up to walk toward the bathroom but instead made my way to his small study at the end of the corridor. I took a breath and collapsed into his small, black office chair.

His Study

His study was the only room in their apartment that was fully his.[11] Very narrow, it was more like a walk-in closet than an actual room. He kept all his books in a small bookcase. Jewish sacred texts: Torah, Mishnah, Tehillim, Talmud; a few philosophy books: René Descartes, John Stuart Mill, Georg Wilhelm Friedrich Hegel; and a couple on statistics, one he'd authored himself. I touched the wooden desk and sniffed the few papers left on it. Here, in his study, away from Miriam, the plants, the tchotchkes, and the guests, I could finally be alone with him. I looked around at the unframed photos adhered to the walls: a large black-and-white photo of his own bar mitzvah, a few photos of me as a young child, a couple of old photos of his parents. Next to the photographs there were several handwritten notes. He wrote them and taped them all around: quotes from the Torah alongside mathematical formulas he'd scribbled that I was unable to decipher. I drank in all this information with half-shut eyes, dreading the idea of going back to the main room. Then, it suddenly occurred to me that I must, absolutely must, find something of his: a souvenir, something concrete and tangible that I could hold onto. And where else could I find it but here, in his study?

I hesitantly opened the drawers of the desk. They were messy, full of medical reports, bills, and bank account information. I pushed these aside, looking for something meaningful. Nothing in the top drawer, nothing in the middle one either. I opened the last drawer. There, behind a small plastic box, I found an old, brown leather folder. It was stuffed with papers, and when I picked it up, they fell and scattered on the floor. I picked them up as fast as I could, my heart racing. *His writings! A folder full of his writings.* Handwritten notes, printed materials, stories, poems, journal entries. Small pieces of brownish paper dated 1965, 1967, 1969, 1976, 1982, 1990, 1994, 2000. I shoved them back into the folder frantically.

"Gilly?" I heard Miriam's metallic voice. She sounded alarmed. She had noticed my absence. "Where are you?" she called again, her tone both hesitant and angry. "Coming," I called back. "I'm in Abba's study." Then silence. I knew my time was running out. She would be here in seconds. *I must take this!* I was thinking fast, my palms getting sweaty. *I can't leave this here. She got his apartment, his savings, his clothes, his car, his time, his name. I deserve his writings.* Quickly, I hid the large folder under my black mourning shirt and rushed back to the hall where my backpack was leaning against the wall.

I could see Miriam talking to a neighbor in the kitchen, beginning to make her way toward the study. *Got to do it now!* I pulled the folder from under my shirt and shoved it quickly into my bag. I felt a shiver down my spine. Miriam noticed me and asked, "What were you doing in the study?"

"Just wanted to be alone for a little while," I answered.

"Please stay in the living room. You have no reason to sniff around the apartment," she said, her expression cold.

"Sniff around?" I asked in disbelief, before our conversation was interrupted by new guests.

The next day, I found the door to his study locked. I was shocked, but I no longer cared. I had all I wanted. I took a deep breath and joined the guests in the living room. For the first time this week, I felt my lingering migraine fading away. I smiled to myself, thinking victoriously: *I did it. I fucking did it. I have his writings. His memories are mine!*

The Tomb

Our shivah, like most shivahs, passed in monotony. Guests came and left, snacks, cold drinks, coffee. Paper plates, paper cups, exhaustion. I settled into the routine. Seven days. Navigating between hours of talking to guests, some of whom I knew well, others not at all, getting snacks, clearing the table, exchanging short words with Miriam, and all this time "being nice."

Judaism is very pragmatic: It outlines clear behaviors and rituals, leaving little room for self-doubt. Every mourner, depending on their relationship to the dead, has a script to follow and all rituals are anticipated and prescript. The shivah is followed by a thirty-day mourning period, after which the grave is visited, the tombstone is set. And so, on day thirty, in alliance with Jewish protocol, which Miriam followed carefully, we gathered again under the beating sun, women on one side, men on the other, as we placed the *matzzevah* (tombstone) over the grave.

Mourners are officially released from their mourning position and may return to daily routines after this ceremony. All except for the children of the deceased, for whom the formal mourning period is extended to a full seven months. That was me. His only child. *Yetomah* (orphaned), I had seven months of mourning ahead of me. And it wasn't a matter of choice; I was following protocol.

Gathered once more at the grave under the unforgiving sun: wife, daughter, brother, his cousins, and the single colleague, we waited for the rabbi to say the Kaddish. This time, we came prepared with ten men for the minyan. And I came prepared with migraine medications, which I took in advance. It was hot, humid, ugly, and miserable. Haim, Miriam, and I hadn't seen each other since the shivah and hadn't even exchanged phone calls. This meeting didn't feel natural. We went through the ceremonial actions, but I could feel that all of us just wanted to be over with it.

The *matzzevah* was placed over the grave. It was engraved: "Yossi ha'ahuv shelano" (Our Beloved Yossi). *What a silly, childish thing to write about an adult*, I thought, as my anger toward Miriam, who never consulted me or made any effort to include me in the decision, bubbled. Her choice of calling him "Yossi" instead of "Yosef" made me fume with anger, but I stayed silent. There was no point in bringing this up; it was too late. Still, my mind kept going: *"Yosef Hochberg" should have appeared on the stone. He was a somebody. Not a random "Yossi" or a little kid to be remembered by his nickname. He was a famous professor, a scientist. A man of great achievements. Not a "Yossi!"*

As I was boiling with rage, Miriam approached me. "You can come get your photos. I put all the photos of you in a bag."

"I will," I answered, surprised that she had spent time getting rid of pictures.

"Do it soon, please," she added. "I am cleaning everything out. And I don't need *those*."

I felt a boiling hatred toward this woman, who had gone from weak and simple to manipulative and mean in just a few weeks. Her words cut through my throat and burned my chest. Held-back tears were blocking my airways. Miriam left, the others walked away, and I began to cry. First, a few dry tears, then a few heavier ones, then sobbing. Fully fledged, shaking, crying, moaning, shivering. This was the first time I'd cried a real cry since he died.

Drifting

I still had four months left for my sabbatical and a lot of research left to do for my book. But none of that seemed to matter now. I dropped all my work obligations and committed myself fully to the performance of proper mourning: visits to the grave, saying the Kaddish, and wearing black. At any rate, I wasn't able to focus or think, so there was nothing else I could do.

I kept myself busy going through these ceremonial acts, but the pain was making its way inward. And as the weeks passed by, I began to feel that reality was drifting away from me, or I from it. Friends and family kept trying to comfort me, telling me how profound it was that I happened to be in Israel at the time of his death:

"He must have known that you were here."

"He must have waited for you to be here."

"At least you were by his side."

Even my seventy-year-old Polish analyst from Los Angeles, whom I'd been seeing for years and with whom I spoke on the phone once a week during my sabbatical, was convinced that me being present at the time of his death was of great importance, "a way to find closure."

Closure? I tried. I really wanted to believe that it mattered that I was there. I desperately wanted to believe that he wanted me to be there and that this was all meaningful. A divine intervention. But I knew this wasn't true. My father had long lost the capacity to make plans, practical or otherwise. I had no illusions. I didn't think he planned anything or "waited for me." I suspect he didn't even know that I was there.

Another month passed. By June, the heat of the Israeli summer was becoming unbearable. I've always hated Tel Aviv's humidity. The air gets heavy and, unless one is a beach person (I certainly am not), there is hardly a place to escape the brutal sun. Moving from the initial shock and the mourning rituals back into a routine was hard. I felt nothing. But this nothingness wasn't just numbness, it was more like evaporation. I was gradually losing my sense of my body and where I was. I knew I was in Tel Aviv and I knew my father died, but instead of having this knowledge translate into an embodied feeling, I was drifting away, my body somehow floating away from me, and I? I wasn't sure what that meant. Without sensing my body or my location, "I" began to mean very little.

I kept going through the motions: parenting my two young children, meeting friends, collecting material for my book, preparing to leave the country, all the while putting great effort into masking the fact that I could hardly hold a sense of the present. I lost orientation and I lost weight. I recognized people who came to offer comfort, childhood friends and relatives I hadn't seen in decades, but they all seemed like phantoms, part of a lingering dream. And I a skeleton wandering in the dark.

Out of Place

Four months passed in rituals, ceremonies, visits to the grave. But these actions didn't help me feel more oriented. The line between reality and fantasy kept slipping away and I was counting the days to leave and return to California. Keri and the kids—all born and raised in the United States—made it clear, each in their own way, that they had enough time exploring this land of blood and conflict. They were most certainly ready to go back to the calmer reality they, but not I, easily called "home."

I never felt at home in Los Angeles, where we had lived since 2002. Nor did I feel at home in Tel Aviv, where I lived from ages six through twenty-seven. If anywhere ever came close to "home," it was Berkeley, where I went to graduate school. Being a small university town, before Google set its headquarters in San Francisco and destroyed the city and the entire Bay Area, Berkeley offered me a sense of comfort. It was far enough from everything I grew up with (war, aggression, my mother's migraines, Israeli machoism), it was peaceful, it was green, and it was filled with coffee shops where people read books and talked about abstract ideas. It was comforting to me.

But "home"? No. I never quite felt at home anywhere. Nor did I particularly enjoy this sense of displacement or being "out of place." Surely not as much as Edward W. Said had, although, like him, I recognize the political importance of "not belonging."[12] I found the experience of feeling mislocated painful, and especially now with my father dead, my sense of belonging and being became totally fragmented. And this despite the fact that we hadn't been close for so many years. And despite the fact that I hadn't lived with him in the same house, or even the same country, for the majority of our lives. Somehow, still, the relationship we had when I was a child was as close as I have ever associated anything with being "home." And now that he was gone, that association was gone too.

Wall in Hebron

Miriam and I hadn't talked since our short and unpleasant exchange at the stone setting. She made it clear that she was moving on (she remarried a year later), and given that I already had the only thing I needed—his writings—I had no desire to contact her either. The only time we met again (and for the last time since) was at the reading of my father's will, the last thing I had to do before going back to Los Angeles.

I had no idea what to expect, but I somehow trusted my father to do the right thing. I was his only child; my two kids, his only grandchildren. Miriam was his wife and his caretaker. His first wife, my mother, was totally uninvolved and planned to keep it that way but even she reassured me, "Abba batu'ach tipel be-zeh" (Your dad surely took care of things).

He wasn't a rich man, just a retired academic, but he owned the large apartment they lived in and had some savings, in addition to whatever was left from his parents after they'd died, including reparations they were both paid by Germany for their suffering under the Nazi occupation of Poland. I assumed Miriam would get the most, as deserved, and myself and my kids the rest.

Five years earlier, during my visit to Israel, my dad mentioned his will. It was the first and last time we ever talked about it. "I want you to know, Gilly, that I took care of everything," he said without any warning. "Miriam will get this apartment and you'll get the wall in Hebron."

"The wall in Hebron?" I asked, astonished.[13]

"Yes," he responded, as if this was a totally normal thing, and continued, "I couldn't buy the whole apartment so we bought it together."

"What? Who? Who is we? What apartment?!" I was thinking that he was beginning to speak in tongues again, expecting a full biblical fantasy to unfold. But no. He continued to speak measuredly, in a calm tone: "I joined three other good Jews. Together we each paid for a fourth of the apartment. So we each get a wall. *Yehudim tovim* [good Jews]."

"What?!" I couldn't believe my ears. At this point I was used to crazy, but not this level crazy. Not from him, not from the other "good Jews." Jewish settlers buy walls in a living unit in Palestinian Hebron? This was news to me. Alarming, sad news. But I also knew he was gone.

I saw no point in having a political discussion with him about this. No point in having any meaningful conversation about anything anymore. Not at this point. We lived in parallel realities and radically different temporalities. He was part of the movement toward building the Third Temple and Judifying the Promised Land. In his mind I was "lost," "living among the goyim in California," "abandoning my roots and my ethno-national-religious commitment to my God, my People, my Land." How do you penetrate this vision that to me was nothing but sheer craziness, madness on a global scale?

I didn't argue, I just said, "I don't want anything to do with that. I would rather you leave me nothing. Please." I tried to keep my voice from shaking, shocked to hear that he actively joined the settlement project in the Palestinian town of Hebron and, even more so, that he didn't even realize the absurdity of his offer. *A wall in Hebron?!*

"Don't be stubborn," he replied. "You can sell it if you don't want it. A wall is a wall. It is property!"

"Thank you, but no thank you," I responded. "I want nothing to do with this property, or quarter of a property. Or with those good Jews. Please."

"As you wish," he concluded. "But you should know, He is watching," he added, pointing toward the ceiling. We never spoke about the will, or the wall, or Hebron again.

And now that I was walking to the lawyer's office in South Tel Aviv, I was hoping he remembered his promise and spared me the burden of having to inherit any portion of this shameful property. Not a wall, not even a stone.

His Will

A narrow, gold frame hanging on the door of the otherwise bare hallway announced: "Mr. Feldman, DL." Miriam was already there when I arrived. We said a quick, dry hello and pressed the buzzer. The door opened and a pale woman in her mid-forties invited us into the office. "Ladies, Mr. Feldman will be right with you," she said, pointing at the two narrow, wooden chairs facing a large oak desk. "Let me get you some water," she added and closed the door behind her.

Miriam and I sat down as far as possible from each other. Even so, her sitting apart was quite different from mine. Hers carried an aura of a final confident victory—she held her body apart from mine. Mine was timid, anxious, and already tainted with defeat. We didn't exchange a word. I could smell her sweet perfume, and it made me nauseated. I looked at her feet in low heels, her blue dress, a red, velvety scarf around her neck, and her overdone facelift. I was surprised to find her looking so put together and elegant. I tried my best to feel empathy. But I couldn't. Everything about her—the professional looks and her fake confidence—agitated me.

A few minutes later, the door opened. Mr. Feldman turned out to be a small, bald man in his mid-sixties. His office was equally small and gray, and the oak desk, which was disproportionately large, made the rest seem particularly squeezed. The secretary walked in with the water. Mr. Feldman shook our hands, coughed, and said, "Let's get right to it." He pulled out my father's will from a sealed envelope and began to read. It took less than a minute, because the will was no longer than a sentence, which read: "I LEAVE EVERYTHING, ALL MY SAVINGS AND BELONGINGS, TO MY LEGAL WIFE MIRIAM HOCHBERG. TO MY DAUGHTER GIL HOCHBERG, I LEAVE MY MOTHER'S SILVER CANDLEHOLDER."

I heard Mr. Feldman's laconic voice reading my father's will with one word ringing repeatedly in my head: *candleholder*.

"That's it, ladies." He put down the paper. "Now you both just need to sign."

I leaned over, looked at Miriam in disbelief, scoffed, and signed. She looked away and signed as well. I stood up, my legs shaking, unable to contain the pain or the shock. I just wanted to get out of there and get as far away from her as possible. Her presence caused me endless pain. No wall was mentioned. No other property either. Nothing. A candleholder. "How could you, abba?" I heard my own voice mumbling, as I got back out to the street. It wasn't just the money I cared about. And I was certainly relieved to not have to deal with the settler's wall. The hurt came from feeling erased, as if his last message to me was: "You don't matter... Our shared past doesn't matter."

"You should stop by the house to pick up the candleholder," Miriam called over, behind me, as she was making her way to her car. "It is silver, you know, pure silver." I never looked back at her. A few days later, just before leaving the country, I sent my brother-from-a-different-father to collect the candleholder.

"It's pure silver," I said and winked when he passed it on to me.

2013–2015

Los Angeles

Mourning and Melancholia

Armed with my grandmother's silver candleholder and the folder of my father's writings, I left Israel and returned to Los Angeles. For the first few weeks back home, I placed the candleholder on the dining table, compelled to light the Shabbat candles, something I've never done before. I thought it would be a gesture of respect, honoring my father and my grandmother. But this ceremony got tired quickly and didn't feel genuine. *Lighting the candles and blessing the Shabbat?* It didn't stick. I was never into observing Shabbat or following any other religious rituals. And Keri and both kids found the whole thing burdensome: "Why do we need to do this?" So, I ended up moving the candleholder into the kitchen closet.

My father's writings I shoved deep into my bedroom closet, hoping to forget about them, at least for a while. I had a life to live, two young children to raise, a career, a book to finish writing. Engaging with his texts would stand in my way. I needed to get back to my life. Besides, what was the point? He was dead. There was no hurry. His writings could wait. I was determined to move on. I did. Until one day I was no longer able to move at all.

Aged forty-five, two years after his death, I suffered a nervous breakdown of sorts. It built slowly, or fast, depending on how far back I trace the warning signs. But in any event, ten pounds lighter and unable to eat or drink, the center didn't hold, and I had no more energy to fake it.

"Acute depressive episode," a psychiatrist in Beverly Hills concluded after an hour-long meeting. I called him "The Cowboy" because the only memorable thing about him was his cowboy boots, an anomaly in Los Angeles, let alone Beverly Hills. Over the course of three months, the cowboy prescribed me ample medications: mood stabilizers, antidepressants, sleeping pills, pills to increase concentration, uppers and downers of all sorts. I took a pill to wake up, a pill to fall asleep, a pill for appetite, a pill to walk, and a pill to talk. Sure enough, I ended up in the emergency room, where they flushed my system of this pharmaceutical orgy, but they couldn't wash away the depression.

I struggled. I didn't want my kids to witness my disintegration. I didn't want anyone to see it. I wanted to melt away, vanish, evaporate, become invisible. And then there was the shame. So much shame. It is hard to escape the shame and stigma of depression. So I—the same person who came out as queer in Tel Aviv back in the early 1990s, when being gay was considered a death sentence, and who soon after came out as anti-Zionist, which is still not a popular view (to say the least) in Israel or even among Jews more broadly—suddenly found myself in the closet.

I worked so hard to conceal my depression. *Hush-hush. No one needed to know.* I continued to teach, attend events on campus, walk the kids to school, meet with colleagues, while dying inside. I was lonely, hurting, and anxious. Still, being open about depression felt too risky.

I had good reasons to be afraid. I witnessed my father's mental illness and how it affected his career, his friendships, his status. He lost the respect of his colleagues and neighbors. He lost his friends. Even his brother spoke about his illness in whispers at family gatherings. And I, his only child, kept it to myself, bearing the shame for his moaning and anguish each time I visited him in the hospital, his face to the wall, embryonically folded into himself.

Now, I felt shame for that past shame, while I was also unable to overcome the new shame I mounted for my own depression. On the face of it, I had no reason to be depressed. I had two joyful, healthy children, a loving partner, close friends, two sweet cats, and a career I loved. Without a doubt, I lived a comfortable, middle-class lifestyle. I had no right to be depressed. This made everything even worse. I felt doubly ashamed.

I was also terrified, and for good reasons. Back in 1991, my father's psychiatrist Dr. Chermesh told me, "I don't want to alarm you, but you should be aware of the fact that bipolar disorder is often heritable." I lived with this warning ever since: examined and evaluated every minor change in my mood, making sure I was reading the signs and diligently staying alert. I sought evaluation with many therapists and psychiatrists, confirming time and time again that I was not like him. But now, depressed as I was, I was terrified that they were all wrong and that I was fulfilling my genetic destiny. *It was inevitable.*

I lived under the shadow of his mental illness. I became convinced that his genes were inside me. It was inescapable. In my twenties, I witnessed his metamorphosis into something I never knew could exist: a monstrous, deflated body without vitality. And now that he was dead, I feared that he, or this thing he had become, was sitting inside of me. *I was becoming him.* The fact that all this was happening to me upon turning forty-five made it even scarier. This was the exact age he was when he became this thing. This lifeless monster. I decided it couldn't be a coincidence. The threat was imminent. I found myself praying to God, the one I never believed in, "Please God, please, don't make me end up like him. Don't make me lose my mind." Still, tragically, while preventing me from being able to connect to anyone else, my depression and the hellish place I inhabited made me feel reconnected to him. Depressed, I kept him alive.

"The melancholic knows *whom* he has lost but not *what* he has lost in them," Sigmund Freud writes.[14] I read it over and over again. The sentence grabbed me. *Did I know what I had lost?* For Freud, melancholia (depression) is the outcome of one's inability, refusal, or failure to mourn. One's inability to accept the loss of a loved object. It is, in other words, a defense mechanism, albeit one that comes with a very heavy price. The melancholic, he suggests, will do anything to keep the beloved alive by internalizing loss. And so, instead of mourning and facing the loss of the other (the beloved one), the depressed loses her own ego. Her entire world "becomes poor and empty."[15]

Was this what was happening to me? Was my depression a refusal, inability, failure to mourn him? I don't know. I will never know. But what I did know was that it was difficult for me to feel grief because I was so angry and disappointed. He left me out of his will, and this after he left me so many times before. I felt betrayed. I lost him time and again: first, to a new wife who didn't approve of our close bond, then to depression, then to mania, then to messianic fever, and finally to death. I was too angry to mourn.

In 2015, less than eighteen months after his death, I published my second academic book, *Visual Occupations*.[16] I dedicated it to him: "To the memory [of] my father, Yosef Hochberg, October 14, 1945–April 29, 2013." With these words, I inscribed my loss on paper, hoping that in rendering it public I was indeed doing the work of mourning. I waited for the pain to come and for me to begin to feel sorrow. But the dedication did quite the opposite. Formal and polite, it only muted it further. It became a crypt: little, black printed letters on a white page, under which I buried my loss again.

Under this dedication I buried him, his memory, his madness, his illness, his depression, his rotting body, as well as my pain, my memories, my love of him, my anguish, my anger, my loss. It marked the beginning of my depression: a failed attempt to mourn.

Freud argues that the melancholic will do *anything* to avoid having to confront the pain of coming to terms with their loss and that, for this reason, they will incorporate the lost object into themselves, by "devouring it."[17] *Was my depression my way of devouring my father?*

By the very end of 2015, after long months of agony, I was beginning to crawl out of my darkest abyss. With the depression slowly shedding off, I became aware, on a corporeal level, that it was time: I had to let him die so I could continue to live. I pulled out his texts, which I had hidden in my closet for some time, and began to read. I was practicing, and it took time to stop devouring him and to instead devour his writing.

2016 | 1976–1985 | 1970–1975

Los Angeles · Ann Arbor & Bloomington · Chapel Hill

Letters

On an early Friday morning in February 2016, I found myself alone at home. I pulled a chair from the kitchen and stood on it, reaching the top shelf of my bedroom closet. I pushed aside the winter clothes, looking for the black plastic bag I'd shoved behind them almost three years earlier.

I lifted it and pulled it out of the closet. It was much heavier than I'd remembered it to be, so I quickly dropped it on the bed. I opened it hesitantly and emptied it on the bed. I wasn't quite ready to engage with any of the writings I found at the shivah; I had no idea what I would find there. But I felt strong enough to reread the letters he'd sent me as a child, between 1975 and 1986, from various university towns in the United States. I was seven when he sent the first letter and seventeen when I received the last.

Most of these letters were written on thin, light blue paper provided by the American postal services. Others are written on university letterheads: NYU, Bloomington, Michigan, Cornell. I began the task of meticulously tracing the order of years, months, weeks, and days. Almost all the envelopes I found were torn—evidence of my eagerness to open them as a child. There was something so magical about our letter exchange: the time gap between the act of writing, sending, receiving, and reading these letters. Like sending secret messages in a bottle. The suspense and faith involved in hoping the message will find its right destination and be read by the intended reader.

My dad handwrote all his letters to me in Hebrew script. Tightly curved letters, small spaces, straight lines, narrow borders, as if he aimed to fit as many words as possible into each page. He opened every single letter with the same phrase, "Yaldati yechidati" (My only girl-child), and signed them all with the words "*Be-ahava*, Abba" (With love, Dad). The word *abba* he wrote in print, while the rest of the letter is all in script. I picked up a random letter from the pile and read:

Feb. 19, 1977

Yaldati yechidati,

I'm such an absent-minded professor. I forgot to send you the two postcards I wrote last week! I just found them yesterday still sitting on my desk. Silly me. I promise to do better. I am also going to record myself and send you a cassette so that you will be able to hear my voice and hear my singing. Bloomington, where I teach this year, is a small town but there is actually a lot to do here. I am planning ahead for your visit. There is a water park not far away and a great pool on campus. I am sure we will have a great summer!

Love, ABBA.

Reading his childlike sentences fills me with tender feelings. He clearly wrote to meet me at my level. I was eight years old when I first read this. Now I reread and imagine her, that child I used to be. I delve into sweet nostalgia, pain and pleasure:

I'm running down the stairway, through our fourth-floor building, down from the third to the lobby, rushing to check the mailbox. My little heart pounding. Will there be a letter from dad? Yes! I can see it through the nar-

Letters from my father's archive, 1976–85.

row opening. I insert my fingers and pull out the blue envelope. I recognize his handwriting. I can barely control my excitement as I run up the stairs, tearing the letter open before I make it to my room and sit on the end of the bed. I'm breathing fast as I begin to decipher his curly letters. I've only very recently learned to read Hebrew, after my mom moved me to Israel with her. I still feel more comfortable speaking English, but I have to be able to read his letter so I try hard. I read slowly, one word at a time. The letter carries a promise: "Summer."

Summers

I lived for summers. I spent summers with my father and away from everything I didn't like: Israeli heat, my classmates, my mom's headaches, and my stepfather, who was actually very kind but still wasn't my dad.

Our summer vacations were filled with fun activities and adventures, and they surely helped bring us close together, but they also meant that our relationship developed like an island separated from the mainland. A world standing on its own. Our secluded world and ours alone. A reality into which we both drifted, just the two of us, every year, like a "perfect couple" for a short time. Then, back to reality.

I waited for summer all year long. Not just for the adventures and activities but for the sense of playfulness it gave me. In this insular alternate reality, I was able to fully embrace fantasy and a sense of freedom. And for me, as a child, this meant, above all, that I was able to finally stop being the girl I was and become (if temporarily) the boy I wanted to be. Enjoying the sweet memories, I picked up another letter. This one is dated October 1, 1978:

> My sweet child! I love you so much and I feel we are going to be a great couple this summer! A father and daughter couple. I have a feeling I know you very well, because you are so much like me and also a little like your mother, too. Yes, the truth is that you took the best from each of us. And this is why you are so lovely! It is strange sometimes when I think of it. How unexpected life can be. I remember the day I met your mom. Time is so mysterious . . . one moment your mother and I were together, and next thing I knew, she was gone, and you were gone with her. It makes me sad to think of this. But enough with this melodrama! I can't wait for you to come visit. We are going to have a great summer together.
>
> Love,
> ABBA

Summer with Dad. Bloomington, Indiana, around 1979–80.

In many ways we were indeed "a great couple," my dad and I, during my childhood, with summer vacation as our only shared time. It was likely easier for us to build a fantasy world together given the limited time we spent with each other. But as a child I didn't think in those terms. I simply divided my reality into two: My mom was "reality principle," with all its soberness, inhibitions, and censorships. My dad was "pleasure principle": dreams, playfulness, freedom, and beyond.[18]

Underwater

One of my favorite activities during my summer visits with my dad was going to the pool. At age seven, I barely knew how to swim, but going to the pool with him was never about swimming. Unlike my mom, who had always gender-policed me, my dad didn't care. He had no issue with me not wearing a bikini top. He never asked anything about it, just let me be. This alone was an occasion for celebration. Without the top, I walked proudly around the entire pool area, looking down my flat, narrow chest and then looking around, imagining everyone thinking, "What a cute boy!"

At last, I was a cute boy in a small swimsuit and the world was mine. I have a vivid memory of one such day. I think we were in Ann Arbor (*or was it Berkeley?*). I must have been seven or eight when we visited a local pool. I remember the feeling of my body melting in the water as if it happened just yesterday:

> *The shallow water hugs my little body. I dip my head in and twist around myself. Once, twice. I can't really swim, but I can float, twist, and turn. I open my eyes, and through my goggles I can see my skinny, bare chest and my skinny legs touching the pool's tiled floor. Hop, hop, I jump. I close my eyes to better see the bump I imagine I have between my legs, under my bathing suit. I circle around myself and imagine my small bump. As long as I am underwater, I know I am totally free. I am a free child circling around herself. Skinny legs, skinny arms, bare chest, small bump. I am such a cute boy. I float and smile.*

This memory fills me with a wave of warmth, even now. My body feels the water as if this just happened. It is touching my chest and my feet are touching the pool's floor. I can even see my father waiting for me at the edge of the pool, smiling and holding a big, blue towel. He lets me stay in the water for a long time, until my lips turn purple. Then he calls me out: "Gilly, time to get out. It's too cold! Let's get you warmed up and go get lunch. Steak and fries!"

It wasn't that my dad was ever part of my dreamy, stolen moments of freedom underwater, or that I shared with him my desire to be a boy, but he never interrupted my dreams, either. He never asked why I wasn't wearing a top and never asked why I referred to myself in the masculine form. He would just let me be me. And when I would ask him, wet and cold out of the water, "Do I look like a boy?" He'd smile and say, "You look like a very *cute* boy!"

Hasidic Hits

The following year, my dad moved from Ann Arbor, Michigan, to teach at the Indiana University Bloomington. I remember this summer as the most glorious one we had. My dad rented a trailer in a park, not far from campus. "It was cheaper than the university apartments," he explained to me. "University housing is full of boring academics. Here it's much more fun! Consider this an upgraded camping experience."

The trailer was so small that one had to bend down to get in. On the right, there was a kitchen with a hot plate, no stove. On the left, two narrow bedrooms and a tiny shower. The living room had orange carpet, green shades, and a brown sofa. I loved it! And I was old enough (at least my dad determined so) to stay alone whenever he went to campus. During those times, I would sleep in late, wake up slowly, eat cereal, and then head out to the nearby playground a few blocks away. It was small but had two swings and a slide. I crossed the grassy area between the trailers, dividing "zone A" and "zone B," every day. And every day I waited with a mix of hope and fear for another kid to show up. I fancied it would be a boy and we would become best friends. We would become inseparable and spend the whole summer together swinging. But no one ever showed up. After a couple of hours of swinging and daydreaming, I would head back to the trailer to read, snack, and wait for my dad to come back and make us one of his notorious dinners. Then the singing would begin.

A typical evening at the trailer involved what my dad called "Abba's magical dinner" followed by listening to Hasidic music, dancing, and singing along. His dinners were magical in the sense that he was able to "make something out of nothing." He hardly ever had anything in the refrigerator, but somehow he always managed to come up with a great meal. "All you need is one meatball, cut in two, a couple of potatoes and one onion, and you got yourself a royal dinner!" After, he'd say, "Shall we listen to some favorites?"

It became a routine, but we pretended it was spontaneous, and in a way it was. "Sure! Let's play some Pirchei London."[19] They were our favorite Hasidic boys' choir. My dad introduced me to them when I was seven. We'd dance to their songs, joining in with their high, pubescent voices, imitating their Ashkenazi-Yiddish-mixed Hebrew.

> Ko amar ko amar ha-shem matzah chen ba-midbar
> matza matza matza chen, matza chen ba-midbar, oh, oh, oh, oh
> Am sridai, sridai harev, am sridai yisrael

> [And so said God, I've chosen you in the desert
> In the desert I chose you, chose, chose, chose
> People, ruined survivors of destruction, chosen]

We sang, danced, and laughed for hours. I'd imitate the lead singer, who was about twelve, whose voice hadn't yet broken. Oh, how much I wanted to be him: a Hasidic boy in a black suit, white tzitzit, and long side curls. I still remember all the lyrics, and sometimes, to entertain friends, I put on my "Hasidic show" and become the young Hasidic boy who lives inside me:

> Ashira la-shem be-chayai, azamra le-elokai be-odi,
> yeruv elav chiki,
> anokhi esmach ba-shem

> [I sing to God with my life, I praise my God with all my being
> My bosom longs for Him
> I find joy in God]

Becoming a Hasidic choirboy was my dream, and with my dad, I got to live it. We both did. I still love imitating the boys' Yiddish intonations.

As I write this memory down, sitting at the kitchen table in sunny Los Angeles forty years later, I smile to myself picturing the scene in my head. I wonder if there was ever any other trailer in Bloomington, Indiana, or elsewhere for that matter, in which a father and daughter spent the evenings together singing and dancing to Hasidic hits.

Free to Be . . . You and Me

Going down memory lane, I realize, perhaps for the first time, how central my childhood bond with my dad was to my queer identity formation. Childhood memories flash before me so vividly and in such detail that I lose myself in them, not without pleasure. Queer pleasure. So many of them are about my past desire (nowadays mostly forgotten) to be a boy. That was how my queerness first manifested, long before I had any idea or understanding of either my gender or sexuality. And it wasn't that he and I ever discussed this directly, more that he gave me the space to fantasize and enact my cross-gender identification without scrutiny and censorship. Being a boy was my dream, and with my father I got to live it.

From the age of four to about ten, I wanted more than anything else to be a boy, which for me meant one thing: growing a penis. I didn't have a precise image of the actual organ in mind yet, but I had a very clear grasp of the noticeable bulge that boys had between their legs and girls did not. *They had. I didn't.* That was the gist of it.

Boys in my kindergarten made jokes about penises frequently. They held peeing competitions in the school's backyard, and I used to sneak behind them to watch. I wanted to be part of those competitions and jokes, but I was only permitted the status of a hidden witness.

One day, Rey, the wildest boy at school, drew a picture of a penis and ran around the class with it until the teacher caught him, ripped his drawing to shreds, and spanked him in front of us. It was 1974, Chapel Hill, North Carolina, a church school, so there was nothing unusual about the spanking. But the image Rey drew tantalized me: a hot dog connected to two balls, one on each side. *Is that what it looks like?* I had to find out.

Steve was my best friend and the only one who defended me when I told everyone I was a boy. By then, I had already successfully passed two tests set up by Rey to prove my masculinity. I stepped on a cockroach and killed it, showing no fear or remorse. And I managed to spit—a big, foamy-saliva spit—while swinging. My spit was so hard, it went far beyond Rey's. This should have affirmed my boyhood beyond all doubt, but some kids still insisted I was a girl. Steve had no doubt. He was always on my side. He never doubted me, not later that day, not ever. Not even after the horrible day when my mom came to school, set all the kids around in a circle, and told everyone, "There appears to have been some sort of a confusion. Gil isn't a boy. She is a girl. She's a lovely girl." Steve just looked at me as she talked. His gentle expression made my shame slightly less painful.

I grew up in the heyday of *Free to Be . . . You and Me*.[20] Most kids raised in the United States of America in the mid-1970s knew the TV show and the popular vinyl. Other than *Mister Rogers' Neighborhood* and *Sesame Street*, there was no show that so dramatically shaped the landscape of 1970s American middle-class childhood. I knew all the lyrics by heart and sang along with the record again and again. I still feel a buzz of excitement remembering the hopeful tunes and the utopian lyrics:

> There's a land that I see where the children are free.
> And I say it ain't far to this land from where we are.

> Take my hand, come with me, where the children are free.
> Come with me, take my hand, and we'll live.²¹

Free to Be... You and Me was the product of 1970s feminism, and its liberating message was clear: Girls don't have to be pretty and boys don't have to be strong. We can all be liberated from the prison of these gender norms.

> When we grow up, will I be pretty?
> Will you be big and strong?

Young Michael Jackson and Roberta Flack asked each other and answered reassuringly:

> Well, I don't care if I'm pretty at all.
> And I don't care if you never get tall.
> I like what I look like, and you're nice small.
> We don't have to change at all!²²

This was all very liberating for me, a little girl growing up in the South wanting to be a boy. But even *Free to Be* left me hanging; there was a limit to its promise. In the land where "the children are free":

> Every boy grows to be his own man [and]
> In this land, every girl grows to be her own woman.²³

I was a little girl, full of hope and dreams, but I didn't want to "grow to be my own woman." I wanted to grow a penis.

I spent days, weeks, months, even years praying. I was convinced that if I prayed hard enough, I would wake up one morning with a small penis between my legs. Sometimes I prayed to Jesus, sometimes to Elohim, depending on the setting. At school it was always Jesus. At home, with my secular Jewish parents, that seemed inappropriate and ineffective. So, at home, alone in my room, I switched to mighty Jehovah, the one and only, who has no son. I didn't discriminate between the two divine forces. I prayed to them both, concluding I had nothing to lose. Better yet, I doubled my chances.

By the time I entered elementary school, I perfected my study of boys' crotches. I used to sneak into the basketball court or the gym just to catch a glimpse of their skinny legs, pretending to look at the games, while fixating on the glorious bulges under their shorts. Tantalized. I stared and imagined that soon enough, I would have the same hump between my two skinny legs. I had no doubt this was only a matter of time and strong will. I was able to spend many blissful hours in my head, alone, in fantasy worlds where I was already a boy.

Walk like a Girl!

Back in 1970s-era Chapel Hill, every birthday party ended with different goody bags given to boys and to girls. Boys got little plastic cars or little model planes. Girls got plastic rings and necklaces. I wouldn't have it! I protested and demanded to get a boy's goody bag at every birthday party I attended. This embarrassed my mom greatly. She spent so many days of my early childhood trying to convince me how wonderful it is to be a beautiful little girl. I had no intention of accepting this or surrendering.

My mom couldn't tolerate my gender transgressions. She didn't just inform my peers I was a girl, embarrassing me and exposing my lie to my entire kindergarten; she was constantly monitoring my gender performance:

"Why do you walk like that? . . . Walk like a girl!

"Talk like a girl!

"Dress like a girl!"

I remember these evocations like scars on my flesh. They are among the few memories I have from my early childhood in Chapel Hill. I grew up there until I was six and a half, when my mom left my father.

After ten years in a turbulent marriage, she decided to flee. While my father was away at a conference, and realizing that a friendly divorce was not an option, she packed two suitcases, got her sister to buy two tickets leaving from Raleigh-Durham Airport to Ben Gurion, Israel, and arranged for a friend to drive us to the airport. I remember none of this. But I know the story.

Over the years, I've looked through the two albums my mom created and titled "Chapel Hill" many times to try to connect to childhood memories, even if they were generated through photographs. I've never been able to find a single photo of all three of us together. Sometimes I wonder if that triangle ever really existed, as it has no traces in my mind.

The memories I have of my parents are always already divided. Me and him versus me and her. It was a split I grew up with but also was invested in. Her policing of me made her the bad breast; his laissez-faire approach made him the good breast.[24] Later I would come to realize that this dichotomy was part of an orchestrated fiction I created as a child and that it was never really true or accurate. But as a child, this split served me well, or at least it made it easier for me to map out my reality: Summer was separated from the school year; United States from Israel; boy me from (forced) girl me.

Me at age six. Chapel Hill, North Carolina, 1975.

I get up and stretch. I pick up the Chapel Hill yellow album (the other is orange), pushing the large pile of my father's letters to the side. I am too far gone to stop this nostalgic journey. My childhood is coming back to me, demanding attention, full stop.

I open the album to a random page and stare at a black-and-white photo of myself, age six. I remember exactly when the photo was taken. I remember everything about that moment, when my mother pressed on the shutter button and I felt magic happen. I see it clearly as I stare right at the child looking back at me with a hint of a victorious smile on her face:

> *Leaned against a lamppost, I am staring into the camera, a big smile on my face. I am looking right at my mom, who's taking the photo. We just got out of the hairdresser. It's my birthday. I have turned six. Finally, I got my long, wavy hair cut. Until then, my mom refused to let me cut my hair. "Your hair*

is too pretty to cut!" But on that day, my sixth birthday, my mom gave in. *"I want a haircut," I responded after my mom asked what I wanted for my birthday. My mom surrendered.*

I look at the photo now. I look closely at my short hair. I remember how euphoric I felt back then. This photo was my trophy. It documents my victory against my mother and the belief I had as a child that the camera's shutter would transform me from girl to boy with a "click."

I know that what my mom doesn't realize when she's taking this photo is that she isn't just taking a picture of "me." She doesn't know my secret: When she takes the photo, magic occurs, and I become a boy!

I believed it, fully. In this sense, the photo is not a simple documentation of my victory over my mom's refusal; it is the ontological victory of my imagination! I knew she had no idea that I was transformed into a boy the minute she pressed on that shutter. And knowing she made the magic happen, without even realizing it, made it all the better.

Click. With the sound of the shutter, I became a boy! It was magic.

And even though I am no longer that dreamy child who believed in magic and fantastical transformation, the photo I stare at now, forty-eight years later, still delivers this promise to me.

For Halloween in 1975, I wanted to dress up as Mr. Rogers, my favorite TV persona. I loved Mr. Rogers and wanted him to be my father, my brother, my mentor, my friend, but equally I wanted *to be* him. When I asked my mom if I could be Mr. Rogers—"All I need is a tie, a dark-red sweater, a...,"—she didn't even let me finish. "If you want to dress up as a boy, fine," she said. "But why not a cute baseball player?"

"I want to be Mr. Rogers!" I insisted. At that point, my mom and I had already spent hours, days, and weeks arguing about my hair, my clothes, my walk, all of which she determined were "too masculine." It was war. But this time my mother won. I ended up in a baseball outfit. "See," she said, "you can be a cute boy. You don't need to dress like a strange old man."

Thinking back, I wonder if my mom unconsciously sensed and feared not so much my desire to be a boy (there are, after all, lots of "cute tomboys") but my attraction to the unconventional and nonnormative. Clearly Mr. Rogers's masculinity was eccentric; he was in fact quite feminine. He was an older man who dressed like a nerdy dandy and took his sweet time changing his shoes for house slippers at the beginning of every show. My mom was okay with me wanting to dress as a "normal" sporty boy but not as what she deemed to be a "a strange old man." Yes, I think it wasn't my desire to be a boy that my mom dreaded so much. It was something else. Something neither of us were aware of yet: my queerness.

Queer Survival

Things were different with my dad. He didn't seem to be bothered, alarmed, or even particularly curious about my transgressive gender identification or expressions. With him, for a short month every year, I was able to be the boy I wanted to be. This was the biggest gift he gave me, without necessarily even knowing he did.

Some of my most vivid memories of the two of us involved make-believe games. During the school year, I played mostly by myself, enacting scenes with imaginary friends, but during the summer I had a partner to play with. My dad and I created a few imaginary games and played them over and over again, summer after summer. Did he initiate them? Did I? I don't know. I don't remember. But as a child, I never felt he played in order to entertain me. He was as much in it as I was. Perhaps he was longing to connect with his childhood self. Perhaps playing was his own psychological coping mechanism (D. W. Winnicott tells us that "in playing, and perhaps only in playing, the child or adult is free").[25] In any event, his love of playing and ability to fully engage in imaginary scenarios matched my childhood desire to flee into fantasy.

There was the giant toilet paper game in which we reenacted a huge roll of toilet paper chasing my dad. The toilet paper was there to avenge my dad's excessive use of paper in the restroom. It came back to "wipe him off the planet." My job was to save him from the giant roll by chasing it away before it "flushed him down the toilet." I'm pretty sure my dad wrote the script.

Other games similarly shared themes of terror, escape, hiding, combat, and rescue. Over the years, I came to understand this was the makeup of his entire inner world. And later in life, when he became sick and delusional, his illness too unfolded a vivid world of biblical enemies, Gog and Magog, prophesies of revenge and redemption, in which he was sometimes the victim and at other times the redeemer. When I was a child, these games were nothing but delightful for me, a playful leap into an imaginary world, both thrilling and comforting. We bonded over them, sharing secret worlds and laughter.

In the gestapo game, we were both partisans, escaping from the secret police. We'd hide behind the sofa pretending to shiver with cold. At some point, my dad would mimic the sound of footsteps approaching. This was the sign that we'd been discovered, so we had to stay as silent and immobile as possible. Behind the sofa, waiting for the danger to pass, we exchanged looks and then, when my dad gave the sign, we jumped from our hiding place and ran through the apartment into the forest beyond (the bedroom). "We made it!" my dad would declare, and we would both holler. "This demands a celebration," he'd say and pour us each a cold glass of Coke. It never occurred to me, then, that my father was reenacting real childhood fears. His parents were both survivors who'd spent most of WWII running from one labor camp to another, hiding in forests, as they made their way from Poland to Russia, to Siberia, to Uzbekistan, to Kazakhstan, where my father was born. But we never spoke about any of this; we just played.

My favorite role-play, without comparison, was Abba Rasha (Mean Dad). We played it for years. Abba Rasha involved a reenactment of a series of events: I'd pretend to break something or drop food on the floor. In response, my dad would grab a broom, approach me with exaggeratedly heavy steps (which made me laugh), and announce in a dramatic tone, "You have been a very bad child! Very, very bad! And you will be punished! Lie down on the bed!" Then he would lift the broom in the air and pretend to spank me with it, saying, "Bad child, bad, bad, bad!" over and over. It would make us both laugh hysterically. When I grew older, and we no longer played the game, we would enjoy talking about it, reminiscing how funny it was. But I think we both sensed something about it was forbidden and "kinky." It was that unspoken part of the game that undoubtably made it so joyful, but we never talked about that either.

My dad was my childhood companion in these tacit secrets of transgression. There was something about his own quirkiness that put me at ease. Unlike my mom, he seemed to have no interest in saving face and couldn't care less about whether I dressed as a boy or girl, or whether he himself followed any normative behaviors. He would teach in shorts and flip-flops, he introduced me to several gay men "because they lived freely," he had hippie girlfriends, and he never missed an opportunity to try new things. "I've eaten everything! Snakes, cats, crocodile, monkeys, and I tried every drug there is out there, at least once," he told me proudly. "Don't ever do anything because others want you to. Only do what *you* want to" was the lesson he taught me early on.

I didn't know or couldn't name my queerness before my twenties; surely I didn't recognize it as a child. Still, there were parts of me I felt comfortable sharing only with my dad. I call those, retrospectively, "my queer parts."

Chilling. NYU apartment, New York, summer 1982.

When in college, I read Freud's "'A Child Is Being Beaten.'"[26] It struck me because Freud writes about a girl's fantasy of being beaten by her father as a sublimation and repression of her desire to be her father's exclusive love object ("I am being beaten by my father because he loves only me"). For Freud, the fantasy reenactment is about repression of a forbidden desire. I read and reflected on the fact that in my world, things looked different: My father and I were openly (and together!) playing out the fantasy, sharing it, staging it, performing it, and enjoying a good laugh about it. The reenactment of what Freud describes as a very common repressed fantasy was anything but repressed for us. It was performative and bonding, and neither myself nor my dad needed analysis to dig it up.[27]

In short, I think that what Freud recognized as "perversity" and analyzed as repressed, forbidden desire (of all girls for their fathers) served as transgressive material we engaged with in a queer performative way, even if neither of us did so intentionally. Freud's "'A Child Is Being Beaten'" became, in our performative rendition, an overt plea: Can this child please be beaten? An invitation, an exchange with another to reenact, face, play out, confront, and subvert with joy.

Role-play, make-believe, theatricality, performativity, reenactment. These are all part of what queer children do not just to survive but also to find pleasure in what heteronormativity and gender norms deem unacceptable, even unimaginable. After all, queer children have to find outlets of expression long before they even know they are queer or know how to express it.

As a preteen and later as a teen, I began to play with friends. I played with my third-grade friend, Iris. Our game didn't have a name or a prescribed script, but it had predetermined roles. Iris was a girl, I was a boy, and we were in love. Playing went like this:

We sit next to each other, usually at her desk, and exchange love notes. We pass them between us, pretending we'd received letters from some faraway land. Iris reads hers first, then I read mine. She jumps around the room, hugging the letter, kissing the paper. I hold her letters with trembling hands, bringing the paper close to my face. And, if I get lucky, Iris becomes superexpressive and runs toward me, leaning forward and giving me a kiss.

Iris and I played at kissing, which meant we got to be bold, pressing our lips together. When she offered me my first "real French kiss," I happily accepted.

A year later, age ten, I began playing with Shelly. She was my age and lived a floor above me in the same building. Our game, which lasted for almost three years, was called "The Feldman Family." Together we invented a whole family: mother, father, and four children. This family inhabited both our apartments and the stairway between them, which became one big penthouse for our large, happy, wealthy fantasy family. In reality, we both lived in small apartments in the same grayish cement building. Neither of us had siblings and neither of us were happy. Shelly lived with her divorced single mother. I lived with my mother, my stepfather, and my mother's migraines. The big family Shelly and I created together was everything we both wanted and didn't have. And for years we reenacted the various dating scenes each of the siblings had by fondling and kissing as we went on fantasy dates.

There were other friends and other pretend games. All of them involved queer transgression. I credit my dad for being the first to introduce me to this mode of playing, where desire, fear, and fantasy come together, whether or not he intended it (I suspect not).

My dad gave me the gift of queer survival two full decades before I read Judith Butler's *Gender Trouble* and realized performativity was a thing.

2016–2017

Los Angeles

Not All Playful

Not all his letters bring back such sweet, playful memories. In the following weeks and months I read all his letters, organized them chronologically, and discovered, to my great surprise (*Was it a disappointment?*), that my childhood memories were (as memories always are) quite selective. The image of my childhood father as my partner in joyful playing and free transgression remains intact, but his letters reveal other sides—sides he chose to openly share with me as a child and I chose to either ignore or forget over time.

Rereading these letters now, as an adult, I see clearly that his inner world was made of far more than singing, playing, and amusement parks. And he made no effort to hide it from me. On the contrary. He wrote to me telling me about his loneliness, his insecurities, his pain. Even when he talked about himself with bravado ("I'm the most famous scholar in my field! You should be proud of your dad!"), he wrapped it up with sadness, almost despair. His melancholia takes me by surprise. I hurt for him. I hurt with him. I hurt for my forgetting.

A single letter, dated June 24, 1980, catches my attention. I calculate the years and realize I was eleven when I first read it.

> Hi, *yalda*. I am in the Big Apple. This is how NYC is called because everything here is big, but also because you have to be careful not to bite on the sour side. You see NYC is like the Garden of Eden: You need to know what not to bite into. Remember the story in Genesis? God told Adam and Eve they can eat everything, just not bite into the fruit of knowledge (it wasn't an apple BTW!). But of course, they were tempted, and they ate it. NYC is just like that: It is a heaven filled with forbidden fruits. And you have to make sure you only bite into the sweet apples and avoid the sour. The city is full of interesting things but also scary things. Pleasant people, but also some unpleasant people. The truth is, I am not used to being in such a big city. And I feel lost here. Lonely and scared. I don't want to lie to you. I am sharing this because I think you are old enough to know that abba is not as brave as he may seem and not as happy as it may look. I am alone here in this big city. So please write to me. Your letters make me feel less lonely.
>
> Love you, ABBA.

PS I promise that by the summer, when you visit, I'll already be an expert in what fruit to eat and which to avoid in this scary city. Together we'll make NYC a safe Garden of Eden!

He felt small and lonely and scared? My dad? Did these words fly over my head when I was eleven? Did I choose to look away and simply stay with the comforting knowledge that by the time I'd arrive he'd be "an expert... and... together we'll make NYC a safe Garden of Eden"?

In the following months, I continued to read his letters and discovered this one wasn't an exception. On the contrary, in later letters, as I got older, he was even more explicit about sharing his pain, his sadness, and his loneliness:

"Your mother broke my heart when she left me.

"I am really great with statistics but not so great with human beings.

"It is hard for me to make friends.

"All my relationships with women are a failure."

I'm astonished to have no recollection of the sadness and insecurities he shared with me. I pick up another letter, this one I received when I was thirteen:

Yaldati yechidati,

It is sometimes hard for me to admit that deep inside I am not a happy person. I am not the joyous and funny abba I appear to be. I am not sure how much of this I should share with you because you are still a child. But I think we need to be open with each other so that together we can learn how to live with fears and anxieties. These feelings are part of life. But I also think that you, my little girl, are smarter than me, and you probably already know everything I have to teach you about fear, anxiety, and sadness. But maybe *you* can teach me something about all this? They say children are the best teachers!

Love,
ABBA

PS When I get very lonely and sad, I remind myself that I have you! I can't wait for the summer to arrive already and for us to be together.

Perhaps I didn't forget. Perhaps I internalized this knowledge and turned it into change. His words must have been burdening to read at thirteen. Perhaps it was this burden that made me, as a mother, so focused on sheltering my kids, who are already in their late teens and don't need my sheltering as much. I want them to feel I am always strong and always able to protect them, even if I know that they know it's impossible. I want to keep them cozied in childhood dreamland. Above all, I want to give them something I never got from either my mom or my dad—the gift of innocence.

Remembering to Forget

My father's gloomy letters make me realize how tricky memory is. I begin to suspect my memories even as they come flashing before me with full details and force. *Are these real? Are they reliable?* Memories are hard to trust. And they're confusing. The more you write, the more you remember. Or think you remember. But you can never be sure if you are remembering or creating memories of things and events that might not have occurred. And whether the memories you remember are there mainly to block other memories you'd rather forget.

My memories of my childhood summers with my father are mostly beautiful. *Did I embellish them because they were part of an alternative reality I created for myself? Did I paint a rosy picture of my father so I'd forget his less appealing sides?* His loneliness, his insecurities, his anger, his restlessness, his impatience, his exaggerations, and his self-grandiosity were surely known to me, but they hardly ever disturbed my pleasant memories of our shared summers. *Do I write what I remember, or do I remember what I write?* I don't know, and to a great degree, I don't care. I even accept that I remember, at least partly, in order to forget. Either way, I am determined to save my tender childhood memories. I am committed to making them part of my present.

Papa Gorilla

I keep reading his letters, looking at family photo albums, and doing everything I can to protect my good childhood memories. He signed one of his early letters "Papa Gorilla." I smile, my chest filled with a gushing, nostalgic, warm ache. My dad was a hairy man. He was covered with dark, thick hair, on his chest, his back, his arms and legs. I would make jokes about it and call him Papa Gorilla, to which he'd respond, "That makes you a baby gorilla."

Papa Gorilla and I used to take bubble baths together until I turned ten or so, before my mom heard about it and put an end to it. Those shared bubbly times were my absolute favorite.

Papa Gorilla. Chapel Hill, North Carolina, 1973.

"It's Papa Gorilla bath time...," my dad would call out from the bathroom. "Cooooooming!" I'd yell back.

> I jump into the tub. He is already in and covered with bubbles. The water is hot. I put some bubbles on my nose, and he makes a fake bubble-beard. We laugh and make fake snowballs to throw at each other. The soft bubbles stick to our hands. When the water gets cold, he gets out and hands me a towel. I see his hairy butt and I laugh. Once I'm out, I sit on the mat next to the bath and look up at him, wet drippy-hairy. I pretend I'm drying myself as I stare and try to see through his towel. I want to see his penis without him noticing that I'm looking. Finally, I get a glimpse of it. It is hairless! I conclude that my dad is a hairy gorilla and his penis is a little snake wandering through the jungle.

In later years, a therapist suggested that these baths must have been confusing for me and that the sight of my father's nakedness was somehow inappropriate, even traumatizing. But I refuse to subject myself to this reconstructed memory (heteronormativity? American Protestantism?). For me, those remain memories of tender moments. Play, joy, and healthy curiosity. I won't let any therapist take that away from me.

First Attempt

By March 2017, I'd spent a year rereading my dad's letters. Avoiding the folder I found at the shivah, filled with his writings, like the plague. I left it untouched, still sealed in the plastic bag. I wanted to prolong my joyful childhood memories as long as I possibly could, and I knew that moving away from his letters and into his later writings meant I would have to confront his illness, his madness, and likely many secrets I sensed I was better off not knowing. I was still in the process of recovering from my own breakdown and feared that engaging with his depression (I anticipated finding it in his personal writings) would push me back into mine. Still, I was feeling pressure mounting. And curiosity. After all, I knew from what little my eyes managed to capture when I first found the folder that it held texts going back several years before I was born. *I would have access to my dad's mind, memories, longing, as he was before he ever knew I would be here.* This thought tantalized me. The idea that my dad was a full person, a young man (a teen!), before my arrival and that I could meet him as he used to be through his writings was not something I was willing to give up. Whether he intended this or not (he didn't), he left me his writings: his thoughts, poems, stories that were older than me. *He was speaking to me from beyond his grave.* I had to listen. And not just listen. Record. I sensed it in my entire body. It wasn't a simple obligation. It was a drive. A call: *I must hold his memories.*

I made my first attempt on March 19, 2017. Alone at home, sitting by the kitchen table in our LA house, I picked up a random paper from the folder. I decided to just pull one out. It was a piece of yellow legal-pad paper, dated April 2000. I read it, following my dad's familiar curly, handwritten Hebrew script, which didn't change much throughout the years. It looked similar to the writings I recognized in his letters, just a bit shakier. *It must have been the medications*, I noted to myself, explaining the slightly fuzzy look of the word and the ink stains. The page is a mess: lines crossed out and others written above them. There are food stains and greasy marks all over the paper. Most of the writing includes quotes he hand-copied from Psalms, but toward the bottom of the page he added a few lines of his own, some of which he circled and underlined with a green marker:

"I thank you, God, for trusting me as your chosen Messiah.

"I trust you will keep your promise to me.

"I am your vessel, so do with me as you please" (*Aseh bee keret'sonkha*).

These writings belong to the version of my father I am less keen to remember. No longer my childhood companion. A madman. I see him writing it now and his image forms before my eyes:

> *He is eating, crumbs falling from his mouth onto the page, then coffee drips. He tries to remove the stain with his hand, only making it messier. He pushes the cup away. He gets agitated. He eats impatiently. He writes, deletes, writes again. His brain is on fire.*

I kept reading for a little longer, feeling my chest getting tighter. "God," "promises," "Messiah," "redemption," "punishments," "omens," and "revelations." His words, scratched out and rewritten, were piling up on the page and coming through my throat. *Enough!* I found myself pushing the paper away, gasping for air. It was too late. These words threw me into a spiraling anxiety. *I am not ready*, I told myself, got up, collected the papers, and shoved them all back into the box, the box inside the big plastic bag, and the bag back into the back of my closet. *Enough for today. Tomorrow I'll try again*, I promised myself. But I won't. Not until another year passes. Not until we move from LA to New York, a city where I spent so many wonderful summers with him.

2018 | 1980–1986

New York

Bleecker Street

So much changed in my life. After fifteen years of living in Los Angeles, hating every minute of it despite truly loving my colleagues and students at UCLA, I had the opportunity to move. I was hired by Columbia University and relocated with Keri and our two preteens to New York City, a place I knew well from childhood, a city I loved and where I immediately felt at ease.

New York City for me was always "my dad's city." Following many years of visiting professorships across the United States, he settled in there, teaching statistics at New York University. This was the best thing that could have happened to me. I was eleven the first time I visited him and stayed in his sublet faculty apartment at Washington Square, then, across the street, at another faculty house on Bleecker Street. He'd always preferred to sublet, never renting his own. "It saves the need to buy furniture," he said. I loved it. It meant that each summer I was surprised with new furniture, books, layout, smells, decor. There was the anthropology professor's living room, which was crowded with African sculptures, the ethnomusicologist who had a grand piano and a remarkable collection of vinyl, the marine biologist whose library was filled with colorful volumes about oceans. Every summer a new apartment, and every summer a new girlfriend. Some I got to know better than others. They came and left, leaving no imprint, from one summer to the next. Neither the apartments nor the girlfriends mattered much to me. As far as I was concerned, New York City was *ours*—his and mine alone.

Together, we explored the city. We visited gospel churches in Harlem, saw Off-Off-Off-Broadway shows, ate in restaurants an Israeli kid back then couldn't have even imagined existed: Nepalese, Cambodian, Korean. It all seemed so unknown, mysterious, and exotic to me. We walked the sweaty streets of SoHo, danced to jazz bands playing in Washington Square Park, and, because my dad thought it was important that I learn about the joy of transgression, we also went to see what he called "transvestites"—the sex workers in the Meatpacking District.

On the days that he had to go into the office or teach, I was allowed to go up and down Bleecker Street. From the corner of Broadway, right by NYU housing where we lived, to Sixth Avenue, and back. "You can walk on Bleecker until I'm back, check out the record store, but stay on Bleecker. And don't go beyond the Sixth!"

I was eleven, then twelve, then thirteen, and Bleecker Street was my kingdom. I knew every store, every corner, every café. I knew the block, and each summer it got to know me: the girl who walks up and down, enters each and every store, buys nothing but a sandwich at Blimpie, my last stop. Located between Sixth and Seventh Avenues, it marked the border of my territory.

There was something about the hot, sticky, dirty air of the city in the summer that made me feel alive. I loved inhaling the smog, which enhanced my sense of independence. I repeated the same walk several times a week, but every time it felt like new and my excitement never diminished. I would start with the record store, going down to the basement, the section I knew best, where

I'd look for David Bowie, Kate Bush, and Roxy Music. Flipped through album covers. Talking Heads, Peter Gabriel, Chaka Khan. An hour passed by easily. I never bought anything. Just looked and pretended I was searching for something specific. On the next level, there were buttons and posters: "All You Need Is Love," "Take a Chill Pill." I loved picking those up and reading them. I did that frequently. Bleecker was my street. These were my stores. I walked my kingdom with pride and joy. Up and down, east to west and back, until I felt ready to go back to the apartment, eat peanut butter directly from the jar, and cool off in the AC. Magic hours alone, before my dad would get back.

We moved to New York City in August, but I hesitated before visiting Bleecker Street. Since it was such a central part of my childhood and my memories of him, I wasn't sure how I would feel. I knew times had changed, the city had changed, the street had changed, and so had I. I wanted to keep my sweet childhood memories intact and protect them from the overbearing force of reality and my cynical adult perspective. I postponed the visit from the Morningside Heights, where I now lived, to downtown for several long months. Until I felt I couldn't avoid it any longer.

On a sunny day in late November, I finally took the train and made my way solo down to the West Village. Bleecker looked nothing like it did when I was a kid. The Chinese restaurant my father and I visited almost daily was gone, the corner pharmacy was gone, the poster and vinyl store gone, the jazz club was replaced with a tourist joint, and on the corner of Sixth Avenue, instead of the old Blimpie shop there was a Banana Republic. I walked back toward Broadway Avenue and sat down by the Picasso sculpture on Bleecker, between the two NYU Silver Towers. I had lived in several different apartments in these buildings over many summers. I used to play down here. Now it seemed so lifeless to me. The statue looked ugly and misplaced, the two buildings gray and dirty. There was no point in staying here. It was painful.

I was ready to go back uptown to 116th and Broadway—the New York City I'd only recently gotten to know. The New York I now live in is a totally different city than the New York I remember from my childhood. The neighborhood around Columbia is nothing like the West Village, which is itself very different these days from the Village of the 1980s. I try to piece together the past and the present, downtown and uptown, his New York of the 1980s and my current city. The dirty subway trains are about the only thing that still glue everything together.

How much I wish he were alive now. I wish I could tell him about all these changes. How much I wish he was alive so I could tell him that his little girl, who visited him every summer when he was professing, ended up, four decades later, in the same city, a professor herself. I think he would have felt very proud.

I Am My Father's Archivist

A few more months into our move to New York, I was seated in my study in our apartment on the ninth floor, looking over Barnard College's dance studio and the main dome of Columbia's old library. I'm not sure what propelled me at that very moment—perhaps it was simply my desire to finish unpacking—but at once, I felt I must organize my father's texts. *They cannot stay in that old brown folder!* I pulled the heavy plastic bag out of storage. Since we moved, it remained in one of the few unopened boxes in my study. *If anything, I will get one more box cleared out*, I encouraged myself. No need to read closely, just organize chronologically and divide to subfield. I was craving a sense of order.

I'd recently bought a beautiful chest of coated steel drawers, in which each of the five drawers has a different color. From bottom to top: red, white, gray, green, blue. I spent the following few weeks dividing his writings according to a color scheme that gave me a sense of peace, as if in color coding the texts I'd make sense of them: early texts (mostly poems from 1965 to 1967) went to the lowest red drawer. It seemed fitting since most were love poems, many of which he wrote to my mother before, or right after, they married. The letters he sent me over a decade I placed in the white drawer, right above the red, thinking white symbolizes the color of most envelopes. In the middle two drawers—the gray and the green—I stored the bulk of his other writings: texts ranging from the late 1980s to the mid-2000s; some joyful, but many gray. And finally, in the top blue drawer, I placed all his later texts, written during the last decade of his life. Many of those dealt with his mental illness. Blue seemed appropriate for such gloomy reflections.

The color arrangement was just the first part of an extended process of archiving, which lasted several long months and included various manual activities, all of which I found to be very soothing. I enjoyed the tactility of preservation: laminating the papers to make sure they stay intact, placing them in envelopes, photographing, digitizing. The idea of protecting his writings from the damage of time filled me with a sense of mission and urgency: *I am saving his memories, saving his thoughts.* Above all, I enjoyed writing over his writing in places where the ink was fading. This felt like going back in time, reviving that early moment of writing. I was writing *with* him, sometimes writing *as* him.

My father's writings archived in five colored drawers. New York, 2024.

In my mind, I was enjoying a new make-believe game: I imagined myself to be a professional archivist, a trained preserver of old manuscripts, committed to order, rigor, and conservation. I spent hours and hours meticulously tracing his words, ironing the paper, labeling the folders. *Everything must be in order!* and *Nothing should escape this archive!* I promised myself, even though I knew very well that archives can never be complete.

My Parents

As I was archiving my father's writings, I found myself often comparing him and my mom and the different trajectories of their lives. Both experienced a midlife crisis at the exact same age: forty-five. But the nature of their crises was radically different. My father ended up losing his job, his health, and his sanity; my mother, meanwhile, left her second marriage, moved from the suburbs to Tel Aviv to fulfill her lifelong dream of living by herself, and began to write and publish poetry. She started living for the first time, while he began to fade into his slow death.

My mom, who is now in her late seventies, looks much younger. Her pale skin is so smooth, I'm surprised by how little it's wrinkled. She never wears makeup, and she dresses like a teen: Converse All Star high-tops, baggy pants, and a T-shirt. She isn't particularly agile, but her mind is sharp and her eyes reveal it. He, by contrast, looked so much older than his age when he died, still young, at sixty-seven. And his mind was far gone, lost to manic delusions at times and depressive hallucinations at others.

This comparison saddens me and makes me feel that my archiving mission is of great importance. I cannot let him vanish without leaving his mark. It is on me to make his voice, his thoughts, as crazy as they may appear, come into light. *He needs me. His writings deserve to be read. I am his witness and his oracle. I'm all he has.* And with time, my archiving mission becomes, in part, about saving his memory from the force of my mom's potential destruction. It is not that she had even tried to make me think less of him, but knowing how much he loved and adored her, and how much she didn't love him back, was enough for me to feel that even postmortem he needed my protection.

My parents, Yosef Hochberg and Ruth (née Katchko), met at Tel Aviv University in 1968. She was a literature student and he studied statistics. He worked at the student service office, helping other students find jobs on campus. When my mom arrived, "the most beautiful woman he had ever seen," my dad was determined to find her a job at the library ("What else for a literature student," he bragged). And sure enough, she got the library job, and he got the girl.

They married three months later. Both were twenty-two and both were looking for a way out of something. She, from a steamy romance with a poet twice her age; he, from the grip of his mother, until then the only woman in his life. They found a promise in each other and overlooked the radically different backgrounds from which they came. She, the third daughter of Russian socialists who settled in Palestine as members of the Halutzim (pioneer) movement, grew up in a middle-class, secular, socialist family and went to a public Zionist school. At the age of twenty, after her compulsory service in the army, she began a heated romance with a famous Hebrew writer who was in his mid-forties. This enfolded her into Israeli bohemia early on, before her mother forced her to "chose between him and her." My mom left him, never forgiving her mother, and never forgetting to tell me about it.

My dad was a son of working-class and uneducated parents who'd escaped from Poland to Russia during the war and met in a labor camp in Kazakhstan, where he was born. From there, they fled to Germany to a displaced persons camp and waited, hoping to return to Poland. They didn't, of course, after finding out, with other Jews, that Poland had no interest in welcoming Jews back. Instead, they were shipped to Palestine, a place they knew about only from prayers and never had any intention to settle in. On arrival, they were sent to a poor neighborhood, Yahud, where they kept chickens and sold eggs.

My parents had little in common, but their initial meeting made them both hopeful for different reasons. They each liked to tell me about that meeting in their own way. My mom always emphasized my father's charm: "He was so charismatic and handsome and self-confident." She always added that his charm made her "overlook their incompatibility." She liked to also add that she "was still madly in love with the older writer" and that she was hoping my dad was her chance to flee that love: "Your dad seemed like the perfect guy; someone I ought to fall in love with. He was funny, very good looking, and . . . I never met anyone so self-assured as him. At twenty-two he told me, 'I am a genius . . . I am going to take the world by storm.' I felt it was worth a try!"

My dad loved to tell me how beautiful and smart my mother was and how he could see "the pain in her eyes." "She was the first woman I ever loved," he would say, "but she was sad and I felt I could make her happy." After they divorced, he would add, "No matter what happened, I still love her. I will always love her."

And less than two years later, I was born. Their marriage lasted for nine years, but it went sour very early on. I have no recollection of their lives together, and my memories of early childhood at home are sparse, but I have heard stories. So many stories. Hers and his. And I had to find ways to reconcile his version ("We had some disagreements, but we always loved each other") and hers ("I never really loved him, and he was impossible to live with. I had to save myself; he was a control freak").

Her stories clouded my much happier childhood memories from the summers I spent with him. *My* dad was nothing like the man *she* describes. Now, with him dead, all I have are my memories and her stories. I struggle to integrate these two. True, he didn't like to spend money, which is why, when I visited, we mostly ate at home. And yes, he could lose his temper. Yes, he could be impatient. But violent? Controlling? No.

My mom often talked about my father's anger problems and his violence. I grew up listening to her stories about their unhappy marriage, his extreme mood swings, and her overall misery living with him. "Leaving him was the best thing I did, for me and for you," she told me more than once, sharing various anecdotes about his implosive behaviors:

"He would get crazy and throw things all over the apartment.

"He would lock himself in the bathroom and threaten to kill himself.

"He would scream at me and then cry, and I had to calm him down."

I always felt I needed to defend him: "He couldn't have been that bad!" "He isn't like that!"

To prove that she was telling me the truth and not exaggerating, she would often return to the pivotal story of "the accident." Not to convince me my dad was all bad—she always reassured me of his love of me and supported our relationship—but to warn me of his dark side and to justify her decision to divorce him and take me away with her.

I think the first time I heard about "the accident" I was around ten. My mom told me the story to explain why she was not happy about me taking a road trip with my father that summer from the East Coast to California. "Your father gets excitable," she said. "I don't like the idea of him driving so far." I've since heard variations of the story on different occasions, but her point was always the same: "When he feels threatened, he can be a dangerous man. *He almost killed us.*"

She liked to precede this story by reminding me how silly she was for "falling prey to his charm" before proceeding to tell me about the dangerous combination of his megalomania, inferiority complex, and temper:

"He thought he was God's gift to humanity.

"He needed to be the best in everything, always number one, and when he wasn't, he would lash out.

"He had tantrums.

"He would throw things.

"He yelled at me a lot.

"The man was crazy and violent."

But the one thing my mother has always been clear about was that he never directed his aggression toward me. Never, except that time of the accident— "The only time he totally lost it," she would say, and the details would follow: "You were five and the three of us were in the car going somewhere on a vacation. He was driving, we were arguing—he accused me of flirting with a colleague of his; he always accused me of flirting with someone. Then, he started to scream that he was going to kill us all. He got so angry, and he was convinced

I'd lied to him. He began to speed up, and the small car (a Beetle) was veering from side to side in the wind. I cried and begged him to please stop the car. I pleaded: 'Yossi, our little girl, Yossi, please stop the car!' But he was totally crazy, in a trancelike state. He just kept pressing on the gas and shouting that this was all my fault and that you were going to die because of me. I was terrified. I really thought we were all going to die."

At this point in the narrative, my mother usually stops and asks, "Did I tell you this before?" to which I respond, "Yes, many times, but please go ahead. I want to hear it again." I always want to hear it again, mostly because I take pleasure in seeing how engrossed she becomes in the memory, so much that I think she is perversely enjoying slowing it down and retelling it. I too am perversely enjoying her reliving the horror. I try to wake up my body to remember this, but nothing ever comes back. The very idea of escaping an almost sure death brings us both a catharsis, so I always invite her to go on:

"Eventually the car skidded, bumped into something, and overturned. Somehow, miraculously, the three of us were hardly harmed. We sat there, in the Beetle, upside down, waiting for the police to come and pull us out. *He tried to kill us, Gilly.* And I was too afraid to say anything, so I lied to the police and said there was a deer running across the street. I said your father tried not to hit it and we ended up flipping the car."

No matter how many times I've heard this story, it always leaves me unsettled. "Tantrums"? Yes, I have some vague memories of him yelling hysterically at my mom. "Anger and violence"? Yes, perhaps I even have a half-blurry memory of him throwing a lamp at the wall. But trying to kill me, kill the three of us? Yes, we are talking about a man who later in life tried to kill himself three times. But still, *to even imagine* that he would have tried to kill me? No. This remains unfathomable.

I opened the poetry drawer (the red one) and pulled out a couple of his early ones. He wrote them to her upon their meeting but never gave them to her. When I told her about these a few days later, her reaction was one of total surprise: "He wrote poetry?! I would never guess he had a poetic bone in him! Such a numbers person..."

I read a few of them. Dated 1968, they are naive and not particularly good. That saddened me even more. *How tragic,* I think to myself, *especially given that she is a poet.* When she later asks to see them, I politely decline: "He chose never to give them to you; I think we ought to respect that." The truth was that I feared her judgment. I knew the poems weren't good; why have her reaffirm this?

My mom never loved him. Nor did she ever love Yaron, the father of my two half brothers, whom she married less than a year after divorcing my father. She left him sixteen years later and never married again. Like a heroine in a nineteenth-century novel, my mom loves to love. And for her, a "love less passionate, melodramatic, and painful than that of Anna Karenina or Natasha Rostova is a love not worth loving." She didn't love the fathers of her children. They bored her. She resented them both for "lacking artistic inspiration" and for trying to "kill her free spirit and force her into a life of domestic, bourgeois mediocrity." Neither of them was as passionate as Alexei Kirillovich Vronsky or as seductive as Anatole Kuragin. Eventually, at forty-five, she escaped, met a famous poet, published several poetry books, then left the poet, met a musician, then left him, and met a painter. She was finally living the life she dreamed of.

Over the following weeks I found several more love poems my dad wrote for her. "Ruti, ha-yafa ba-nashim" (Ruth, the most beautiful of all women), he wrote in a poem burdened with poetic clichés. It pained me to read these, and there were so many of them. *How strange*, I thought, *for him to have written so many poems about her but never for her.* She didn't even know he wrote poetry! He wrote these for himself and kept the papers, which miraculously survived six decades, and somehow I became the sole addressee of his love words. He didn't know it, but the poetry he wrote about my mom seems to have actually been written for me.

1972–1976

Chapel Hill

Time Makes a Story Out of Pain

I read almost all his poems. Some of the ones that weren't about her were better. I decided that it might be more worthwhile for me to move on to reading his prose. *If he is anything like me (and unlike her), his prose will be better than his poetry*, I reassured myself. So I closed the red drawer (poetry) and opened the green one (early prose). Among these early texts, I found a fourteen-page document. I pulled it out because it was the longest I'd found. *A treasure.* Dated 1974, written in Chapel Hill, it's entitled, "The Betrayal."

Beautiful horizontal lines of his meticulously compressed small, round Hebrew script cover the pages. Some sections are crossed out with new words written on top of them. He used blue, black, and red pens to write notes in the narrow margins of the pages and sent arrows to sections he circled, adding a little star and a note to himself: "Cut and keep for later" or "Move to section six" or "Get rid of this?"

Having his writing from a precomputer time means that I have access to all his cuts and pastes. His entire editing process is visible; it is part of the texture of the text. All traces of his writing, erasing, rewriting, replacing, cutting are equally materialized. And this gives the writing life. His handwritten text is alive. This is not a synthetic, clean printout; it is, rather, a page full of passion, traces of ink, cross-outs, regrets, and revisions. I can see the places he pressed harder with the pen, his doubts, the words he deleted, and those he replaced.

With a fresh cup of coffee, I took the fourteen pages with me and left the study to read them in my bedroom. "The Betrayal." Early on, I realized I was reading my father's description of the man with whom my mom would soon have an affair—an affair that would break his heart or, as my mother would argue, "his ego."

He wrote about the first time he and my mom met the man who would later become her lover, Amos. I am mesmerized by his careful, almost erotic depiction of this man. The scene: an evening in which four eager Israeli graduate students and their wives were hosted by an admired Israeli professor and his wife.

> The Lipschitzs, the Friedlanders, and the Liebermans were already there. All of them were his students. They worshipped him. I was the only one who wasn't his student. He sat at the corner of the room, smoking his pipe, looking at us all from afar. His wife B sat on the other side of the room, frozen. She eventually tried to break the tension, getting up and offering us snacks. Her eyes kept searching for his. But he just sat there, in his chair, quietly ignoring her. Ruti was talking to the other wives. Amos didn't look at any of us. He seemed tired and disengaged. Still, he was beautiful, transfixing. From time to time, he'd lift his eyes and send a short angelic smile to the group. His lips were parted and his whole face lit up momentarily. His smiles were fleeting, and when they vanished, it felt like we were all gathered just for those fleeting smiles. Like sudden miracles. Between smiles, he collapsed into disengaged silence in the corner, like a gorgeous, alienated idol.

"A gorgeous, alienated idol." How beautifully he wrote about this mysterious man with his "fleeting smiles." I continued to read, mesmerized both by Amos's mysterious beauty and my dad's rhythmic, measured prose:

> The second time we met, Amos sat, just like he did the first time, in his corner. A quiet, untouchable, beautiful sphinx. His head was tilted to the side, his bright blue eyes looked contemplative, and his facial expression had that unique combination of seeming attentive yet detached. It gave him an aura of a man trying to solve a profound riddle. And his beauty . . . such classical beauty. Like a Greek statue. Israeli men never look like that. He was different. He carried a secret, and his movements were gentle, calculated, almost feminine.

My English translation of my father's text doesn't do justice to his original poetic expression. I marvel at the tenderness and eroticism with which he wrote about this man. A man who became my mother's lover and who eventually brought my father so much agony. He doesn't write about the affair, only about Amos's beauty, as if he too was cast under his spell. Then he jumps to his final sentence without mentioning my mother. He simply writes: "Many years have passed since. Time made a story of what was once an old pain."

Time made a story of what was once an old pain. I never knew he wrote, not like this. I didn't know he had such a way with words. I think about his death and what it meant for me. It was, for the longest time, "pain." I had no words to describe it. It lived inside my body like cancer and grew day by day. Pain itself cannot be narrated. It can barely be accessed, surely not verbally. It requires time to help transform it into something that can be articulated. Time gives pain a shape and a form; it makes it into a story.

Page eight was missing. He numbered the pages, one through fourteen, on the top right corner and kept the pages together. But eight was nowhere to be found. I looked everywhere. Was it lost or did he destroy it? I soon began to speculate and found myself creating a narrative about the missing page: *He was in love with Amos, like my mother. He wanted this Greek idol. He must have destroyed the page that contained evidence of that.* Yes. I convinced myself that this is the most likely explanation. A page doesn't just disappear. Surely not from the middle of a text. He must have destroyed it.

Tantalized by the idea that my father had a secret homosexual desire, I decided to ask my mother, the only person who would possibly know anything about it or about any potential homosexual desires he may have had in the past. I told her about the long text I found and about the passionate, erotic depictions of Amos.

"Amos was exceptionally beautiful," she confirmed. "I had an affair with him."

"I know that. You've told me that in the past. But interestingly enough, Dad doesn't actually write about it."

"He doesn't?" She seemed genuinely surprised and more than a little disappointed. "What *does* he write about, then?"

"Mostly he describes Amos. Passionately."

"He was probably jealous. Amos was brilliant, gorgeous, charismatic... All men were jealous of him."

"Well, that is one possible reading," I responded, "but perhaps he was attracted to him?"

"Your dad?! To Amos?!" My mom's voice raised, and she seemed totally astonished. Then she giggled nervously and added, "I really don't think so, Gilly. That would have required an artistic sensibility of the kind he didn't have."

An artistic sensibility. I repeated the words in my mind. When I came out to her, two decades earlier, she didn't seem to think of homosexuality in these terms. She simply called it "perverse."

My mother's admiration of Amos, her noticeably excited body language when mentioning their affair, and above all her blunt dismissal of my dad struck a chord. I found myself rising to my father's defense. "Why do you speak about him with so much contempt! He loved you!" I yelled, "You broke his heart! You betrayed him!"

My mom's expression changed drastically from playful to anger. "He made me miserable. He wanted to control me. He was no man [Hu lo haya gever]."

He was no man. My mom, a poet, never ceases to surprise me with her word choices. No matter how well I know her, and how many times I am faced with her unceasing romantic worldview, heteronormative as can be, I find it astonishing that at seventy-seven she still holds to fairytale-like narratives of passionate love in which "real men" make women feel like "real women." I anticipated the rest of her sentence: "I wanted love and romance. He gave me neither. And he was a terrible lover."

My mom, I told myself, as I have many times before and after, is still like a young girl getting ready for prom, only the prince changes every decade. My father was no prince. He was a simple man, from a simple family, from a small town, who grew up in a yeshiva and still talked to his mother on the phone every day. In Yiddish at that.

"I never betrayed your father!" My mother concluded our heated conversation. "I simply made the decision to not betray myself."

I Am the Guard

I spent a few more days looking desperately for the missing page. It wasn't just that I wanted to find it to prove my theory of my father's latent homosexuality. (I was indeed eager to confirm this, as much as I was eager to confirm his mother's latent lesbianism, about which I, like my two cousins, was firmly convinced.) It was also that I felt he needed my protection. I needed his full story so that I could protect him, protect "it." I was not going to allow my mother's narrative to control my memories of him and surely not to silence his narrative. She was alive, she was a poet, she was gifted with words, she liked to talk about the past. He was dead, I never knew he wrote until after his death, he never shared any of these memories with me. It was on me to keep his memories alive. It was on me to keep a record. It was on me to channel his voice.

Filled with a sense of carrying on a great, important task, my archiving mission swallowed me up. *I must not let him die without leaving his mark. He cannot be left out. It is on me to make his voice heard. He needs me. Intended or not, he left me his writings and I thus became his witness. I am his oracle. I'm all he's got.*

I had a sense of vocation. But I was also aware of the fact that I needed to learn how to witness his pain without it consuming me. I had been there before and had no desire to be there ever again. It was in this context that the most mundane acts involved in archiving helped: Cataloging and preservation not only protected his papers and memories but also served as a shield to protect mine. They helped me put his emotional chaos into order, and I knew well that as long as I was in charge of ordering the chaos, I was safe. I was the maker and the keeper of his archive. I was the guard. We were both safe.

Family Albums, 1968–1974

It was time for me to take a little break from his painful writings and from her stabbing words. Photos tell us different stories, and the photos of my parents' youth presented a much richer and more complex story of those early years than what I could find in either of their verbal accounts.

I picked up a thin, blue leather album with golden letters engraved on the cover: "Yossi and Ruti's Wedding, 1968, Tel Aviv." Looking through the pages of black-and-white photos, I couldn't help but notice the striking difference in their expressions: my father is glowing. My mother, however, looks distressed. Her smile seems forced and her eyes unmistakably sad. His parents, Tsipe and Hirschel, stand by his side. They look so short and fragile and out of place across from her mother, Zehava, a plump Russian Jew who has a big grin on her face. Her arm is resting on my mom's shoulder and she captures the attention of the camera's lens. This is *her* event. I knew, from my mom's stories, that Zehava was greatly relieved when my mother met my dad and left the old writer for him. She hated the idea that her twenty-one-year-old daughter was having a steamy affair with a forty-five-year-old bohemian writer. "Yossi," she determined, "was a much more suitable match, both in age and in manners." The photos reveal her content. She appears victorious in each and every one of these photographs. Her daughter, by contrast, looks defeated or, at best, blasé.

I closed the wedding album and picked up the lighter, smaller honeymoon one. It is yellow and my mom had written "Yerach d'vash" (Honeymoon) on the front page. I recognize her smooth, curly handwriting. They are in Greece. Most of the photos are in color, and both my parents look much happier. They are on an adventure. For my mom, this would be the first trip overseas. My dad had already traveled, several years beforehand, on a youth delegation to the United Nations.

Both of them look young, glamorous, beautiful, maybe even in love. They are posing: he's on deck leaning backward, looking like Alain Delon in a striped T-shirt and a French beret. She's leaning on him, large, white-framed sunglasses covering most of her face, her long, brownish hair floating toward the horizon. His smile shows a set of perfect white teeth, his dark complexion and sideburns give him the aura of an artist or perhaps a sailor. She looks mysterious and fashionable, like Brigitte Bardot. I enjoy these photos. They tell a sweet love story of youth, which likely lasted no longer than the three-week honeymoon.

They must have hired a photographer, because so many of the images look professional, staged, and kitschy: On the boat, he is a sailor holding the mast; at the Acropolis, they are both leaning against the ruins, one on each side; at a tavern, they hold their drinks high up as they stare at the sunset. In most of the photos, he holds her tight against his chest, she's smiling at him, her eyes full of admiration. They're so fine. So dreamy. I would be born eighteen months later. I stare at these people, soon to become my parents, and wish I could have met them back then, when they were young, hip, carefree, and had no idea what a disastrous relationship they were entering.

The last album I owned, "Chapel Hill, 1972–1976," is very different. The dissonance between the glamorous images of my parents at the Acropolis and the snapshots of the family in Chapel Hill is striking. There are very few photos with both my parents in the frame. There are several photos of my dad, alone, mostly shirtless, either sitting by the kitchen table or lying in bed. I suspect I took those in my small shaky childish hands because they are all out of focus. The rest are of me and my mom. She's beautiful, slim, fashionable, but she looks quite unhappy. She's no longer posing.

My parents' wedding. Tel Aviv, 1968.

I look back at my parents' honeymoon album. They look so beautiful and hopeful. But very soon, as revealed in the other album, they would both look tired—crushed, even. I knew they were unhappy; surely my mother was miserable. She never failed to remind me of that. She even shared that sexually, too, she was never satisfied with him: "He had problems. He was impotent." Sometimes she followed this with a semijoke: "Frankly, Gilly, you are a miracle! I mean *literally so*. I have no idea how I even got pregnant."

She and Mary, two virgin mothers. Which made both Jesus and me real miracles.

Jesus

Jesus played a central role in my life during childhood. My parents, two young Israelis who came to North Carolina in the early 1970s without much money, sent me to a local Christian preschool and then kindergarten because that was the only one they could afford. Besides, they saw no harm in me "mixing up a little with the local tradition." They were there because my father was getting his PhD in statistics at the University of North Carolina. My mom made the most of the four years they spent there. She got her master's in education and

My parents' honeymoon. Greece, 1968.

My parents. Chapel Hill, North Carolina, 1972.

had several steamy affairs with men she met at college, which, as she later told me, "made her life with my dad more bearable."

At home, they spoke Hebrew and mainly mingled with other Israeli families—graduate students and the like. With me, they soon had to switch to English because, once in school, I more or less forgot my Hebrew. I forgot many things given that I was not even three years old when we left Israel. I very quickly forgot all about the various Jewish holidays and Israeli marked days (memorials for the fallen soldiers and celebrations for military victories) and adopted what came to be my natural childhood habitat in North Carolina: fried chicken, hushpuppies, corn, grits, church, and, above all, Jesus.

My school was set behind the main church and had a large backyard filled with swings, crosses, and mini statues of baby Jesus. I loved it. I loved my friends, I loved my teachers, and, like the rest, I loved Jesus. We all did. The nicest thing about it was that he loved us back.

"Jesus loves you," our teachers would say every time before we ate. "Jesus loves you," they would say before we closed our little eyes for a nap. "Jesus loves you," they reminded us when we'd go out to play. "Be respectful to each other. Play nicely. Remember, we are all God's children. Jesus loves us all."

There was something comforting about how this love framed my childhood friendships. We were all equally loved by the one we all equally loved back. Perhaps this early setting is what prepared me for my lifelong comfort with polyamory, not necessarily as a sexual practice but as a structure of love and relationships. The monopoly of "one love" never made sense to me. Jesus loves us all and we all love him back, and this love we share binds us together in love. And even as I grew older and realized that "Jesus wasn't mine" (both my parents were keen on making me realize this early on), that "we don't believe in him," that "there is only one God and he doesn't (cannot!) have a son," *"that* God doesn't love you," and, as they hammered it down repeatedly, "you are a Jew!" I never shook off the lesson of pluralistic love as I understood it: Jesus loves us all *and* so that we can love us all *and* love is bountiful. The more of it there is, the stronger it grows. I loved Jesus. We loved Jesus. He loved me. He loved us. We loved each other, or at least we had to try to, because that is what love meant: sharing it and bathing in it.

As a young child, I talked about Jesus a lot. He was my best friend. But from early on, I'd noticed that my parents weren't excited about this, and it baffled me. My mom was gentle about it. She didn't want to confuse me or make my experience at school unpleasant, so she never overtly dismissed Jesus. But she would say, "It is great to have imaginary friends. Is Jesus your best imaginary friend? Do you have others?" I thought she was silly, but I remember thinking it was her special way to think about Jesus, who was, as we learned in school, "invisible" because he was "everywhere, all the time."

My dad was less kind about it. He offered no explanations but simply told me, "We don't talk about Jesus at home!" I didn't like to see my dad angry. It scared me. He could become very upset and scream and toss things. So I learned to keep my love for Jesus at school to share with my teachers and friends, just not with my parents. I didn't know or try to understand or inquire about this; I simply accepted the fact that Jesus was popular at school but not so much at home. I maintained this division carefully. Until the day I slipped.

Per usual, at the end of the school day we all sat on the front steps of the church, waiting to be picked up: Steve, John, Kathy, Mary, and the other kids. Cars pulled up, one by one, and our teacher, whom we called "Big Steve," called out, "John, your mom's here!" "Billy, your mom!" Always moms. I don't remember ever seeing a dad at after-school pickup.

That day, when I recognized our blue car, Big Steve yelled my name: "Gilly, your mom!" But no, it wasn't her, it was my dad! He got out of the car and walked toward us. I was so surprised, ecstatic, and proud. My dad came to get me! I grabbed my backpack and ran toward him, jumping right into his arms.

"Abba! I love you! Jesus loves you!" The words flew out of my mouth before I had a chance to take them back.

A fierce moment of silence followed, then my dad said, "What did you say?" His eyes pierced me and somehow this anger felt familiar, but I couldn't place it.

"I don't know. Sorry, abba," I mumbled.

He kept staring at me, then looked at Big Steve, then back at me and said, "Tell me what you just said."

"I, I, I said … I said that I love you." My voice was shaking.

"And?" My dad's eyes cut through me. "What else did you say?"

"I said … " Tears coming down my cheeks now. "I said that Jesus loves you."

"Yes," my dad said, "and what did I tell you about Jesus?! We'll talk about this at home."

I walked to the car with my head bent down in shame. I sat in silence in the back seat, holding back tears. We didn't exchange a word until we got home. "This damn school! This stupid Black church! I told your mom this is a bad idea. Another one of her stupid ideas!" My dad threw the car keys on the kitchen table. "Sit down!" he barked. "Sit right here. On the sofa!" I'd never seen him so angry, not at me, only at her. "Jesus, huh?" He towered over me, his body blocking the TV. "Listen to me carefully, very carefully. We're going to put an end to this damn Jesus! You are going to learn *ALL ABOUT* Jesus," he hissed. "I'm going to show you who Jesus really is. And after that, I don't want to ever hear his name again. Clear?!"

"Yes," I whispered, choking on my tears.

My dad pointed at the boxy TV behind him. He turned it on and said, "Look closely now," then he turned the TV off. A little white flickering line appeared in the middle, before it became a small dot at the center. Then the screen turned black.

"Did you see that?" He looked at me and smiled. "Did you see that little white dot that disappeared?"

"Yes," I whispered again.

"That's Jesus!" he said forcefully.

I nodded in agreement.

My dad bent down and held my trembling hands. He was finally warm and loving again. "Listen carefully, *yalda sheli*," he said, this time softly, "Jesus was a nobody who thought he was a somebody." Then he invited me to repeat those words: Jesus was a nobody who thought he was a somebody. "Now louder!" he said, and we both screamed out in unison: "JESUS WAS A NOBODY, A NOBODY, A NOOOOOOOOBODY!"

I never mentioned Jesus again.

2020–2022

New York

Visiting the Archive at the Time of Pandemic

Seven years had passed since my father died. By now I'd finished setting up his archive in my small study at home, every text placed in the appropriate drawer, sealed in the right folder, dated, and sorted thematically. His archive was set in place, but I was moving on.

So much had changed in my life. I couldn't drown in the past and didn't want to get lost in his mad writings. So I let it be. Between the summer of 2018 and May 2020, I never once looked at his texts. Life was happening: I started a new job at Columbia University, the children became teens, and we all had to adjust to transition from the slow, sleepy life in Los Angeles to the fast-paced life in New York City. I entered perimenopause, I had a major, urgent spine surgery from which I was just recovering, and I was writing my third book on Palestine, which ironically (or not) was about the need to move away from the historical incentive to engage in archives of the past, toward the creation of alternative archives of the future. Life went on, and I appreciated it.

I moved along with it, leaving my father's archive behind. Then came March 2020. Life in New York City, like many other places in the world, stopped. When COVID-19 hit, the city shut down, and, like many others, I was listening to the never-ending sounds of ambulance sirens and anxiously watching news reports. Most of my friends and colleagues fled the city, which was terrorized by reports of hundreds of deaths every day. We stayed put; the four of us, more or less locked inside our apartment. Columbia University and the entire neighborhood had become a ghost town, with all students evacuated and dorms emptied out.

After a couple of months of shock, isolated at home, terrified, still dealing with pain from my surgery, agitated, and looking for things to do to pass the time, I realized this could be my opportunity to finally delve into my father's archive. As the lockdown continued from days, to weeks, to months, to years, I spent more and more time with my father: his memory, his ghostly presence, his writings. Tucked in my study for hours a day, reading him, taking notes, deciphering the sections that were hard to read due to paper decay and the excessive messiness of his writings felt particularly fulfilling during this worldwide state of emergency: I was saving him from fading away into the abyss of oblivion.

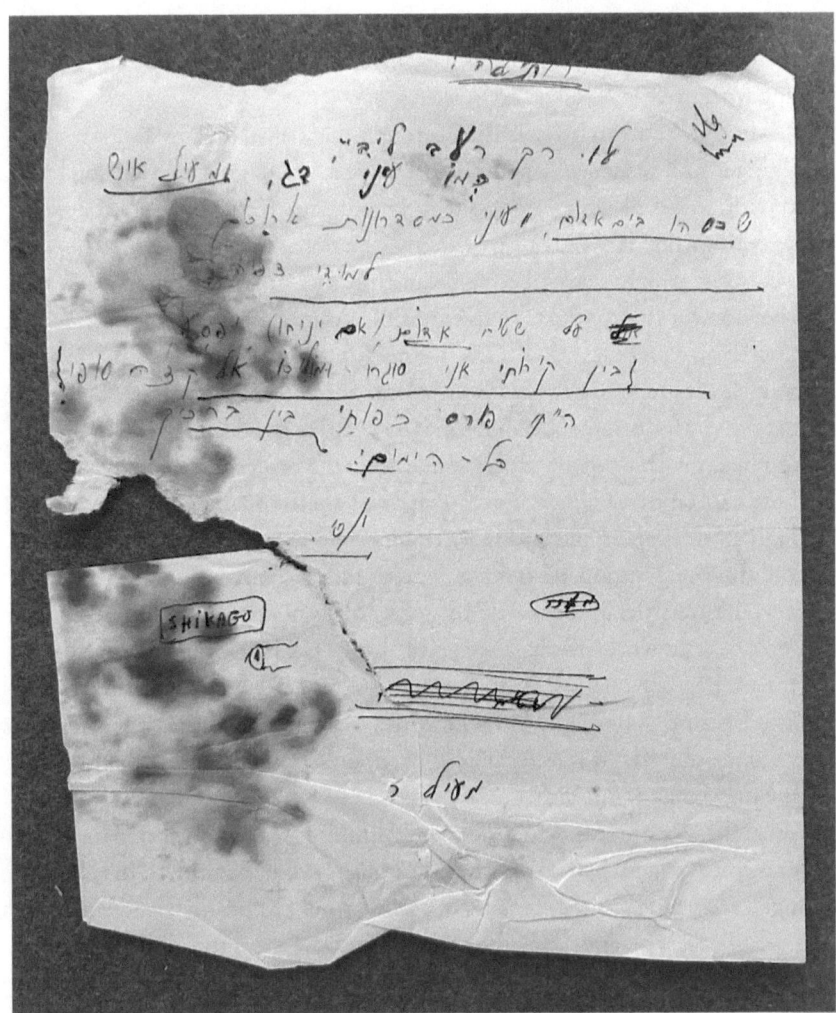

"Decay."

    I looked at the colorful drawer cabinet to my left where I'd meticulously archived his writings. Above it, I kept a stack of his photos. Both papers and photos were at the mercy of time and decay. Decay is part of life, of material, of memory. The pandemic, the closures, and the rising death toll made me realize how fragile all of this was. I made a commitment to preserve everything I had of his: faded images, his handwritten notes, his photographed smile, the curves of his letters, the stains on the papers. It wasn't enough that I'd cataloged everything. I now needed to make sure his texts were digitized and that every single one was laminated. I spent almost all day every day with him, alone in my study, taking care of keeping his past alive. Soon I came to realize that I was playing with fire.

When you are an archivist, sifting through the words, dreams, fantasies, stories, images, and secrets of someone close to you, someone you loved and identified with, someone who is not quite fully separated from you, not yet at least, you're taking a big risk. This kind of archival work has nothing to do with scholarly yearning, which is described so beautifully by Carolyn Steedman as "a specific passion for the past" or "an irrepressible desire to return to the origin," as captured by Jacques Derrida.[28] This is something quite different. If anything, it is about the desire to have a future with someone you have lost. It's not a search for the past or for origins. It's about magic: keeping the dead alive.

You begin with a pile of papers. But unlike the professional archivist, none of these can be considered "junk." You must methodically and patiently go through all the papers, old and new. You have no formal system to follow and no tools for preservation. This is a private, domestic archive, and my dad, while a known biostatistician, was certainly not a public figure. And I, his only child, had no one with whom to share either the joy or the pain of my discoveries.

His archive, the one I've created, is mine alone. There is something strange about it because, supposedly, the whole idea of an archive is that it sets materials in some order that facilitates the use of the collection by others. Archives are made by and for communities.

My archiving process, while rich and fulfilling, felt lonely. I remained the only visitor to this archive I'd created. The glue I used, the folders, the clips are arranged according to my own sense of order. I fixed, traced, filed, and labeled. It was not a process of embracing the archive's dust or "the impossibility of things disappearing, or going away, or being gone."[29] Not because there is any less dust in my father's files than there might be in the nineteenth-century archives Steedman visits, but because the traces I search for belong not to capital-*H* History but only to the dust remaining of my family's personal story.

In this family archive, there is no file more important than another. There is no hidden gem in the dust. Each piece of paper, each word, written or erased, is part of the puzzle: *Who was my dad? What happened to him? Where did my childhood hero go? How did we grow apart? How did he stop being a scientist and become the Messiah?* If I lose one piece, I lose it all.

I was burning mad with archive fever. Soon enough, I realized that when your archive holds your own memories, it has its own life. You begin the process with an illusion of mastery, led by a burning ache for answers, but soon enough the archive takes over and burns you. It dictates the order of things. You end up not only with the memories you wanted to find but also with those on the lookout for you. Like this memory that crept up on me, uninvited:

> *I live with my mother in a small apartment in a suburb just outside Tel Aviv. "Where is dad?" I ask her. "When is he joining us?" By now we've been in Israel for several months already, and a new man is in the house. His name is Yaron. He sleeps in my mom's bedroom. He is here every day. Why is he here? Why is he living with us?*
>
> *"When is dad coming?" I ask again.*

At seven, I was waiting for my dad to join us. After all, I was just swept away from my life in Chapel Hill with no explanation and brought to Israel, where I had to learn to speak Hebrew and adjust to the bully mentality of the kids in school, a kind of in-your-face aggression I was not yet accustomed to. I clung to my mother's promise: "Abba will join us soon."

In our apartment, there was a narrow closet room where my mom kept our winter clothes. One day, coming back from school, I entered it, curious to find all the clothes still covered in plastic shopping bags. Intrigued, I poked in. Among the winter clothes, I found a familiar pair of pants: my dad's light-brown corduroys. I was elated. This was proof of his promised arrival. *Why else would she ship his pants to Israel?* For the following days and weeks, I made a habit of sneaking into the closet, squeezing my little body into the narrow space, and touching the corduroy. Eventually, I dragged them out of the plastic wrapper. I hid them at the side of the closet and came back to hold them in secret every day. It became a ritual. The more time that passed, the less convinced I was of his arrival, and the more attached I became to his pants, the sliver of a fading promise.

Over time, I realized he wasn't coming and lost interest in the corduroy, which no longer carried a magical value. I pulled them out from the secret corner and gave them to my mom, who suggested I bring them with me when I visited my dad in the summer. I didn't want to. Instead, I shoved the pants into my closet, determined to forget about them. I did that for a while. Until one day when I saw the brown corduroys tucked behind my shorts and decided to pull them out and cut them into narrow strips, creating corduroy noodles. It kept me busy for a while. Eventually I collected all the noodles and threw them out. Somehow I knew this act marked an end of an era. I was no longer a naive child, and I no longer believed in happy endings.

Reading, Writing; Past, Present

The pandemic became the routine. I got used to the new, insular reality: teaching online, having both kids at home, my partner losing her job, all of us watching more TV than we ever had. We traveled out of New York City whenever we could to keep our spirits up. But at some point, it became clear that this "emergency situation" wasn't going away anytime soon. I was, like everyone else, stuck at home. I had lots of time and felt I had no more excuses. It was time for me to engage with his texts at a deeper level. I couldn't just continue to preserve them. I needed to read them. Closely. A risky task for anyone, I realized, but especially for me. I didn't want to merge with him and his mental illness in a way that would result in another nervous breakdown. Still, I felt a gripping urge to delve into his writings, to figure him out, this man I thought I once knew and then kept losing.

My reading wasn't passive. In many cases, his handwriting was so shaky or blurred due to the mark of time that I again found myself tracing his handwriting with mine. This became a sensual, meditative, and corporeal act that enabled me to feel close to him but still protective of myself. Our merging was now intentional, and for the most part it felt good. I read/wrote *with him*. We were writing together. His writing, my writing. His writings to me, his writings about writing, his writing about my writings, and my writings about his writing. I soon began writing *back*: writing *to* him, *about* him, *with* him. This was becoming a long love letter. And an echo of despair through which the borders between us were coming undone: archive and archivist, father and daughter, his writings, mine, the past and the present, him, I.

He was dead and I was his only living witness. Along the way, the more I read and the more I wrote, I discovered that I was also writing about myself: my childhood, my sexuality, my gender, and above all about queer intimacy. His and mine. A special father-daughter bond, for which I found no preexisting models.

As a young child, I had to labor to read the Hebrew letters he'd sent me. I spent hours deciphering word by word. More than forty years later, I reread his Hebrew texts with ease but labored on the strange task of translating them into English. The hardest thing was to capture the loving spirit of his words and his humor. He used Hebrew in such a playful way, always making references to earlier registers of language: biblical, rabbinic. Everything he knew from his upbringing in a yeshiva. As a child, I couldn't have deciphered any of this, but I sensed the love and the humor somehow, intuitively.

It was hard to translate these different registers into English. Almost a futile task. *Why am I doing this? Am I hoping to recapture the memories of my lost childhood and fuse those with new understandings?* I realized this was part of it. But neither documentation nor editorial improvement were the point. No. My task was to literally revive those moments. To extend the past into my present. I wanted to make his writing, his words, and our shared past part of my "now." Translating him was my way of *writing with him* and making him and our exchanges of the past part of the flesh of my present.

When the French essayist Roland Barthes looked at a portrait of his dead mother as a young girl, he concluded that every photograph contains the sign of death. The photo affirmed his mother as a subject who is no longer.[30] When I looked at my father's handwriting, I too felt these traces strongly, but for me they were not signs of death but of life. *His fingers left these marks; his hands held this paper.* The curve of the letters, the diagonal leftward slant of his writing brought him back. He was alive in the materiality of his blue-scripted letters. I see the coffee drops. The purplish stain. *What was he eating?*

Reading him, tracing his words, and translating him into English—my language of writing—I joined these traces. I followed his steps. He left them for someone to follow. He writes, I translate, we are writing together. He, I. Then and now. Past and present. This merging is also a separation. For the first years after my father died, I wanted to keep him alive inside me, and the only way I knew how to do that was by becoming depressed like him. Now, in writing with him, I was learning to separate from him, but even more so, I was learning how to keep him alive without having to die.

Lost and Found in the Archive

It has been several years since I began working on this text, and I'm still not sure what it is. Do I need to know? All I know is that this is my attempt to grieve. Or maybe it's actually my refusal to grieve, because as long as I continue to write about him, and keep editing my words, I'm keeping him nearby.

One often visits an archive looking for specific information and answers but ends up with new and unexpected ones. I came into this archival project taking on the process of archiving my father with a clear goal in mind: I wanted to create order and make sense of my father. Above all, I wanted to catalog and keep intact my "two dads": the young and healthy dad of my childhood—my hero, best friend, and partner to secrets and mischief—and the old, sick, and crazy dad of my adulthood whose madness terrified me. I wanted to keep these two dads separated and far apart. Coming into this archival project, I had a narra-

"I am disappointed that you aren't writing me." Letter from my dad, 1982.

tive to protect: "My dad was perfect when I was a child until he had a sudden nervous breakdown at age forty-five and became a totally different person." In my mind, this was the story of his fall from glory, and I had a riddle to solve: I needed to find out why this happened, and I was convinced that if I read everything he ever wrote, I would surely find the answer. Along the way, being his reader, archivist, and cowriter, I would, in the spirit of Athena, rebirth myself out of his head.

But his archive, like all archives, had other plans. My original nostalgic drive tried to push them out of the way. Above all, I wanted to prolong the image of my father as the source of my childhood happiness, because I knew my mother surely wasn't. But as I read on, this fantasy began to fade. As did the strict split I created in my young mind between my mother (bad breast) and my father (good breast). I had to admit to myself that she wasn't all migraines and depression; he wasn't all joy and comfort.[31]

The archive I created failed me. It took away my fantasy of his sudden fall and continued to challenge my childhood memories of comfort and playfulness. I had to come to terms with the fact that my starting point was wrong: I never had two dads. He was always one and split as such: always caught in between, going back and forth between fantasies of grandeur and a profound depression. He was "the king of Yahud," "the chosen son," and "the most brilliant statistician." Yet deep inside, he felt he was nothing at all. His depression was always there, everywhere. Now I could no longer not see it: It is present in so many of the letters he sent me, in his poems, in his stories, really in almost every one of his texts. This made me realize how desperate I must have been as a child to cling to the fantasy of him as "the happy half" of my parents. I wanted and needed to believe it so badly that, until I reread his letters, four decades later, I had no memory of him ever sharing any agony with me beforehand. Discovering that I invented my childhood dad hurts. I sometimes wish I could go back and unread him. I want my memories back, false as they might have been. Instead, I am confronted with information and memories I never wanted to have.

I picked up a particularly painful journal entry he wrote. There was no date on the page, but his age allowed me to conclude it was written in 1983. I was fourteen, and back then, in my young mind, he was my joyful hero. It hurt to burst a childhood fantasy and replace nostalgia with reality:

> I just turned forty. The age of Dostoyevsky's protagonist from *Notes from the Underground*. I identify with him so much. I lived forty years of suffocating self-reflection, injured by the absence of love, the absence of interest, the absence of

passion. Forty years of living dead. I am a walking dead man. All I have is my career and my academic success that comes so easily to me that I cannot see how it could possibly matter. I am a small man: small head, small body, small dick. I am nothing who wants to be everything.

How painful it was to read this and feel the cruelty with which he described himself. How lonely he must have felt, how little self-compassion he had. I forced myself to continue to read despite myself:

I had many women I didn't love. I used them to push away my loneliness. Sometimes sex was good, but it never lasted. I felt nothing. Loved no-one. And soon enough time began to play its tricks. I lost my libido. I visited psychiatrists and I talked to my girlfriends about what happens to me "between fucks." I learned everything was in my hands and nothing was in my hands. I learned women were nothing, sex was nothing, books were nothing, my research was nothing, my success was nothing. I surrendered and decided to let time teach me everything I had to learn about loneliness. Then I learned time too was nothing.

It broke my heart to read this. I never thought of my father as so profoundly depressed. I never thought of anyone close to me as so deeply depressed, not growing up. A child's mind sees things differently. I lived with the image of him being happy before what I considered to be his "sudden fall." Reading these words shattered my world. I picked up another journal entry and very soon regretted it. It was dateless again, but all I could think to myself was: *Why? Why did he write it? Why did I read it? Why am I translating it? Rewriting it?* I didn't have answers, but I was compelled. It was part of his archive. A part I wished I could hide but could not:

I am restless. Can't find peace. I can't read, can't focus, can't even listen to music. No one else knows how I feel; they think I'm always cheerful. I hide my pain. All I have left is masturbation. I use the toilet for that. I don't feel a thing for the women I have sex with. Easier for me to fantasize about them and touch myself. I come and come and come. No passion in my body, just shit, sperm, and sorrow.

I felt slightly sick. Perhaps I was just tired. Something about spending so many hours with his depression made me nauseated. And now this masturbation scene. Before I knew it, I rushed to the bathroom to vomit.

My Father's Penis

If there was something that caught me off guard, something I did not expect to find, and most certainly was not on the lookout for when I set up his archive and committed myself to reading through it, it was his penis. But there it was, time and again. At first, I tried to ignore it. But the more I read, the less possible it became. There are years in which he writes about it excessively:

> My mom forced me to sleep with my hands over my head so I wouldn't touch my penis.
> I hate that I have a small dick.
> My penis gets hard easily but it doesn't stay erect for long.
> I come too quickly.
> Why does my penis tilt to the left?
> When I am lonely, I touch my penis, and for a few minutes I forget my pain.

I kept reading and, for the most part, I was able to ignore these comments. What else could I do with them? But then I landed on a short personal account that sent me off into a spiral of emotions and discharged memories. I couldn't ignore it even if I wanted to. The note is undated, but I recognize the names of the women mentioned, all past girlfriends from sometime between 1984 and 1986.

> I go to the toilet and look at the small mirror. Then I lower my pants down and begin to masturbate. Ahhh... What a good feeling. The heat spreading down there. In my head I am going through images of my girls' asses. I fuck them as I please. I am thinking now: *Who am I in the mood for tonight?* Now I take a short break so that I don't come too quickly. I want to prolong my pleasure. *Michal? Oh, Michaleh, how much you love it when I put you on my stick and talk dirty to you.* I feel my penis getting very hard so I take a little short break again. *Oh Yael, maybe Yael tonight? She breathes so heavily, and drips saliva from her mouth like a beast when I fuck her. I never know if she really comes.* Break again. *Maybe Tsila. Yah, I am in the mood for Tsila tonight. She will go down on her knees and suck my cock with her sweet mouth while gently touching my balls with her fingers*... ahh. My penis is so hard. Another break. I don't want to come yet. After I come, I get depressed. The phone rings. I drag myself to the phone, while still caressing my dick with one hand. "Hello," I say, as cum drips over my arm.

I read. Not once, not twice, but over and over again. *He wrote this to himself,* I noted and wondered, *Who writes such scenes about themselves for themselves?* But then again, he was writing to himself about his masturbation. In some ways, this makes perfect sense. Masturbatory writing about masturbation. *His writing about it to himself is a kind of doubling up the masturbatory action*, I thought, and I congratulated myself for being so clever.

Something compelled me to read and reread this single page. I read, and I asked myself, *Why am I reading this? Am I disgusted? Am I aroused?* It was a pleasant-unpleasant combination. With each reading, the initial shock faded, and I noticed that I was trying to recapture if not recreate that tantalizing sensation I experienced the first time I read it. This thin line between appropriate and inappropriate, safety and danger, pleasure and disgust is the territory of my imagination. And my curiosity. Surely, he didn't think or expect his daughter would ever read this. Reading his text, I became a voyeur. Now *I* am writing about his writing about his masturbation. *I am joining my father's masturbation. We are masturbating. Masturbatory writing and reading. Passing on masturbation.*

Unable to shake off his words or the image for days and weeks, I finally told a friend about it. "Oh, you must read Nancy Miller's text," she said. "If you're writing about your dad *in that way*, then you really must read it. She also writes about her dad's penis." I immediately went online and found it, hoping, above all, to find a sister in crime, someone to share the burden of having to experience and witness her father's masturbation, given that I was no longer able to shake the image, which by now was firmly printed in my mind.

In "My Father's Penis," a chapter in her 1991 book *Getting Personal*, Nancy K. Miller, like many other daughters, grapples with the figure of The Father and, more specifically, with the intersection of penis, father, phallus, and authority.[32] I read Miller's chapter a few times. I liked it, but it left me feeling lonely and, worse, inappropriate. It affirmed what I felt and feared most: I'm a perverse writer in a long lineage of perverse writers. But unlike them, I don't want perversity to define my writing. I am no Jean Genet, Georges Bataille, or Kathy Acker; I want to be a pervert in disguise. I was hoping to find in Miller's "My Father's Penis" some echo, some reflection on my own experience of writing about *my* father's penis. But I didn't.

Miller writes from the position of a dignified, middle-aged woman who has to hold her old father's penis so he can urinate. His penis is "soft and a little clammy."[33] It's an old, sick, deflated penis. I was writing about a very different penis. Miller's dad's penis is a urine vessel; my dad's penis is a sexual organ. She is a caretaker; I am a voyeur. There was no crime in Miller's text and no sex. My shame remained mine alone.

In my mind, I witnessed my dad masturbating again and again. Was this a compulsion fed by disgust or attraction? I wondered how all of this informed and was informed by my queerness. Was my need to witness this repeatedly a matter of cross-gender identification, or was it my ongoing struggle to dismantle masculinity and its hold on me? I couldn't help but reflect back about my childhood penis envy. *Is that what this is about?*

My father's writings, sealed in a box, like a child masturbating in secret, were not meant for me to read. His erect penis forced itself on my psyche as an unwanted and uninvited postmortem gift, but I too entered the scene uninvited. I was an intruding guest. My own transgression, peeking and sneaking around his texts, led me there. His secrets had already become mine. It was the first time I realized just how dangerous it could be to delve into the writings of the dead.

My father's penis spoke to me from beyond his grave, and suddenly my own secrets surfaced. A memory I thought I was done with, a memory I worked through, over and over, in many therapy sessions with many different therapists forced itself on me in full potency and great detail. My nine-year-old self presented herself urgently.

Involuntary memories don't ask for permission; they are invasive and bodily. When the body remembers, there is no point in resisting. I surrendered and became my nine-year-old self again. The compulsion to write and share took over. Sharing secrets: his, mine, ours. Our secrets were no longer set apart.

Uninvited Memories

It was the summer break of 1978. I was nine. My mother and stepfather informed me that my seventeen-year-old stepcousin Mikhael was going to spend a week with us. I was ecstatic. Mikhael was charismatic, handsome, and played the guitar. He represented a world of coolness beyond my reach. He never paid attention to me. But this week, I'd get to spend the days alone with him when my mom and Yaron were at work. This meant he'd have no choice but to notice me.

Mikhael arrived on an early morning the following week. He looked like a rock star, with his black hair, deep brown eyes, and a guitar over his shoulder. For the first couple of days, he was busy clearing our attic above the hallway. It served as a storage space where my mom dumped everything. I spent most of the day watching him feverishly throw things down. "Watch out!" he yelled and threw down a bag full of old clothes. Then a heater, a lamp, some old blankets, an empty suitcase. Everything came down in a storm.

"This is such an awesome space!" he affirmed. "I can't believe how they cluttered this space with so much junk! I'm going to make a palace up here!"

Looking up at him, I was in awe. He was sweating and I was watching the sweat collect on his chest, his underarms, his forehead. He was everything I wanted. I wanted his attention. I wanted him to notice me. I wanted to be just like him. Strong, tall, dreamy.

On the third day, Mikhael invited me up to see the palace he created: "You gotta see this space! Come check this out. Come up here!"

"Do you want some water?" I asked, shocked to hear my own voice and wondering where this mature initiative came from.

"That would be great!" he yelled from above. I ran to the kitchen and filled a glass with water, then added some ice. I was excited to be part of this summer task. "I'll come down to drink," Mikhael yelled and wiped his forehead with a piece of fabric. Then he added, "Hey, no, actually, wanna come up here? Come up here. It's totally cool. You gotta see this space! Come check this out."

"Sh-sure," I answered, afraid of climbing that high but embarrassed to admit so. "How do I get up there?" I asked.

He pointed down to the right. "You just climb over this chair and then hold the side of the door and pull yourself up. I'll help you. It's easy. Just stand up here, and hold my hand... Yes, yes, leg here, I got you! Now jump!"

Whoop! I was up. The attic was just big enough for us both to stand bent forward.

"Isn't this cool?" he asked, looked at me, and added: "From now on this can be our secret space." *A secret place. Mikhael and I share a secret place.* I was hardly able to contain my excitement. "Let's get comfortable," he said and invited me to sit on the floor and lean on a pillow. "Come closer," he directed me to sit by his side. "Do you want me to show you something interesting?"

"Yeah, sure," I responded. *A secret hiding place. Mikhael and I had a secret hiding place.*

"Can you promise you'd never say a word about it to anyone? It has to be a secret. Top secret!"

Top secret. I was so excited; we moved from having a secret place to sharing a top secret. "Top secret!" I said, then saluted.

We both laughed. He leaned over, looked me in the eyes and pulled me closer to him. Then, as he continued to look at me, he pulled down his pants to his knees. I looked straight at the site of action. I said nothing. I just kept looking. He stopped for a few seconds and then pulled down his boxers, just enough for me to see his erect penis.

"Do you want to touch it?" he asked.

"I don't know," I replied.

"Only if you want to." Mikhael's voice came to me from afar, but he'd already put my hand in his and placed both our hands on his erect penis. His hand over mine, he began to move us up and down. His penis felt warm and hard. Mikhael pressed my little hand with his strong fingers closing over it. His breath got heavy. My hand, gripped by his hand, was still moving up and down, but I was no longer connected to it. I just watched it move. A couple of minutes later, he made a choking sound and I felt something warm and sticky dripping down my fingers. He released my hand. I looked down and saw white goo. My heart was beating fast. I began to feel my hand again and realized these were my fingers. "Here," Mikhael said and grabbed a napkin and cleaned my hand.

"I don't like this sticky thing," I said coming back to my body. "I want to go down now."

"Sure," Mikhael replied, and helped me get down before I ran to wash my hands in the bathroom.

For the remaining days of his visit, this ritual repeated itself with little variations. Every day he invited me up to our secret place. Every day I said, "I'll come up, but only if there is no white, sticky thing." Every day he promised there would be none of that. Then, he'd break his promise. Sometimes the white, sticky thing ended up on my fingers, sometimes in my hair, sometimes on my face, or in my mouth. And every time, I followed my part: I got upset, I asked to go down, I went to wash it off.

At night, in my bed alone, I began to put my hands between my legs and touch myself in ways I'd never done before. Sometimes I would see Mikhael's erect penis or the terrible white, sticky thing. I'd try to move the images away. But touching felt good, and the images became an inseparable part of it. I learned to please myself in their shadow.

What was I thinking back then? I wasn't. I did what most kids who are sexually violated do: I morphed into a seducer to overcome the much worse realization that I'd been seduced.

I am terribly shaken by this memory, which invades me at this moment. The flashback mixes up with my father's writing and makes the experience significantly more horrible and unpleasant: Mikhael's cum, my father's cum. I realize that my premature, coerced exposure to sex is suddenly mixed in my mind with my dad's own frustration with sex. I am disgusted.

I cannot shake this unpleasant blending away, and, even worse, it somehow feels familiar, as if my sexuality has always already been mixed with his. I am nauseated by this realization as it takes hold of my body. I am forced to reckon with the fact that this is surely not the first time I find myself feeling confused, implicated, somehow involved. I am faced with the horror of the realization that somehow there had always been a blurry line crisscrossing and indirectly connecting my dad's sexuality and my own.

I pick up my father's note and read it again. This time not so much as a child who had been exposed to her father's sexual secrets and intimate frustration but as a child who was forced to re-remember what might have never been a secret at all.

Shame, disgust, arousal. He and I had always been partners in crime.

I am no longer captain of this ship, I think to myself, realizing my planned writing about his writing has once again become writing about myself. And only a minute or two later, I come to realize how ironic (yet all too appropriate!) it is that I used this term, given that the second uninvited memory that forces itself upon me and demands my full attention took place with him on a boat.

Summer on a Boat

The summer right after I had my unfortunate sexual awakening, my father told me that "this year we will have a different summer vacation." It meant that instead of my usual visits to American college towns, where we spent the month together swimming, taking road trips to nearby amusement parks, eating lots of ice cream, watching films, singing, dancing, and mostly spending time with just the two of us, *this* summer of 1979 we were going to take a boat trip and travel through Turkey and Greece. "You'll love it!" my dad reassured me when I expressed my disappointment. "We'll spend two weeks on a boat, we'll see different islands, we'll swim in the sea, eat all kinds of food you've never heard of before, and I'll tell you all about Greek mythology and the Roman Empire!"

After a long back-and-forth with my mother, who had to agree for me to fly on my own from Tel Aviv to Istanbul to meet him there, the trip was set. When I landed, I was escorted by a flight attendant who helped me find him. What my dad failed to mention to me or my mom was the fact that two women would also be joining us for our two-week vacation.

I was used to waiting for him in airports, but not in Istanbul, so initially upon seeing the two smiling, young women by his side, I assumed this was part of the local tradition. I jumped into his arms and gave him a big hug. He smiled his big, warm smile, kissed me, squeezed my little body, put me back on the ground, and then turned to his side and said: "Gilly, this is Rachel and this is Dafni. They are colleagues of mine and good friends, and they'll be joining us for the trip." Rachel and Dafni smiled and said, "We are going to have so much fun together! Your dad told us all about you!"

I was shocked. I remember feeling my blood dropping from my face all the way to my feet, like my heart was sinking. *Why*, was all I could think. *Why are these two women here?* This was supposed to be *our* summer vacation. Me and him. We never had others join us. True, whenever I visited there would be, at times, some women. They came and left. I would meet them before I went to bed or when I woke up in the morning, but they never stood in my way or threatened my special time with my father. It was clear to me, and I assumed it was clear to him, that summers were ours. Friends, colleagues, and lovers came and went, sometimes joining us for dinner or to see a film, but for me they were all background. Nothing more than stage decoration in a play in which my father and I were the sole actors.

Why then are these two colleagues joining us on the boat, where there is nowhere for them to leave to? My facial expression must have revealed my disappointment as the brunette one, Rachel, bent down and whispered in my ear, "Don't worry, sweetie pie. We are going to have lots of fun together! I promise you."

Rachel was skinny and had curly hair. She seemed friendly and smiled at me all the time. Dafni was slightly heavier. She was a redhead, and I decided she was shier because she hardly spoke to me. *They're both pretty*, I thought to myself as I accepted the news of them joining us, realizing there was nothing I could really do about it. *They are nice. It's going to be fun*, I reassured myself.

The four of us headed out of the airport to the marina. We'd be cruising from one island to another for the next two weeks, spending a couple of days in each place. Soon enough, I realized I hated being on the boat. I was seasick almost the whole time. When we got to land, I was relieved, but I hated the heat, disliked the food, and was bored to the core with archaeology.

"Do we really need to see all these old temples?" I asked my dad, who was holding my hand, dragging me from one sight to another.

"I know this isn't like the waterparks we usually go to," he answered, smiling, "but this is history, Gilly. Mythology! Great human achievements! It is important."

I enjoyed the beach more, and I also enjoyed the few days we spent in Istanbul, from which I carry a distinct memory of the smell of meat and leather. But the trip overall was a painful experience for me, and not only because of my sickness on the boat, the heat, the forced archaeological lessons I had to bear, or the fact that there were no amusement parks and no American candies. What made this trip truly and painfully an unpleasant experience for me were the sleeping arrangements my dad had come up with.

We had two rooms on the boat. I was assigned one, the colleagues were assigned the other. My dad promised me that I'd never sleep alone in the room but insisted that "the adults have to rotate." Every night, one colleague came to

Dad and me. Istanbul, 1978.

sleep in my room, while my dad stayed in the other. They would switch: Rachel one night, Dafni the other. I was confused about this arrangement. I wanted him to sleep in my room. "They're our guests," he told me. "It isn't polite. We each have to host one of them every night." That was his explanation. I wasn't convinced. I was bitter and hurt and decided I had to take things into my own hands. After a whole week passed, I came up to Dafni and Rachel and told them it was his birthday (it wasn't) and that I was preparing a surprise party in my room, which required him to sleep there and wake up to the surprise. It worked. I felt victorious. Whether he liked it or not, that night my dad shared the room with me. I woke up early in the morning and decorated the room with layers and layers of toilet paper, the only thing I could find.

"Happy birthday, Dad!" I woke him up singing. We both laughed, and I sensed my dad knew very well that I knew it wasn't really his birthday. I am pretty sure he understood my plotting. His laughter reassured me. *From now on*, I told myself, *he'll be sleeping in my room*. I was wrong. The next night my dad went back to the original sleeping arrangement, promising to spend the last night of the trip in my room. I don't remember whether he did.

We never talked about it, and I'm not sure what I told myself about this whole situation back then, but I know that even at age ten, I was not naive or stupid enough to believe Rachel and Dafni were his colleagues: They were too young, too pretty, and too chatty to be professors of statistics. I saw how he behaved around them. Sitting between them on the deck, each in a small bikini, he would make silly jokes, grab their waists, and get hard. Yes, I noticed that. By ten I had enough of my own sexual experience to notice that as he stood there in his tight mustard-colored bathing suit that hugged his thin, hairy frame and accentuated his tight, small butt. I knew very well that those two women weren't his colleagues. I didn't even think they were his girlfriends. I wish I were more the innocent ten-year-old he likely thought I was, but I wasn't. I had a clear sense of what was going on. And I didn't like it.

I've asked myself many times in the past, usually prompted by one therapist or another, if borders were ever explicitly crossed between my father and me. "Has he ever been inappropriately sexual with you?" The answer is a definite no. Never. Still, I saw, heard, and knew too much for a young child to not feel that some borders were crossed. I heard him having sex in the sublets he rented. I heard his groans followed by exaggerated, high-pitched female screaming. I knew there were women he paid for sex and others he had actual relationships with, but rarely did those relationships last long.

Whether he intended for this to happen or not (I suspect not), I witnessed many of his failed relationships with women and his struggles with sexuality. I tagged along as an invisible partner to his sexual adventures and both of us—child and adult, father and daughter—pretended that I didn't know what was going on. But I did, sort of. I was exposed to more than I could have possibly fully understood or processed at a young age. It confused me, but I learned to associate certain sounds with sex. By the time I had sex for the first time, I wasn't sure if I should groan or scream or do both.

Writing Memory

When you read a written document or see a photo, you know it's real, at least in the sense that it is there. But when you remember? Memory blends, confuses, wounds, and heals. It is hard to trust. How many of these childhood memories, memories of him, of me, of us, are "real"? How much can I rely on my memory? Images flick by, I see full scenes, remember entire dialogues, places, smells, sounds, even bodily sensations. *Am I remembering a past gone or generating a past that hasn't happened, not fully?* I think about this often.

It is not just that one can never be sure if one's memories are real or fully accurate. The matter gets complicated by writing. Patricia Hampl writes beautifully about this: "No memoirist writes for long without experiencing an unsettling disbelief about the reliability of memory, a hunch that memory is not, after all, just memory."[34] Indeed, attempting to write from and about one's memories is never just about putting recollections on paper. Writing *generates* memories.

It is February 2022, spring semester, and the first few weeks of being back on campus after three semesters of teaching online. We are all getting used to "normality" again, but nothing feels normal. How could it? New York City alone has had so many losses, so many deaths, and it still feels like a ghost town. Students are nervous. Faculty are nervous. We crave normalcy, but we are fearful, anxious, and suspicious of it all: "Is it safe? Can we take off our masks? Should we be sitting so close to each other?" As we come out of our cocoons, it is as if we forgot what it was like to run into each other in the hallways. What it was like to engage in small talk. We crave and fear intimacy. After all, we have all spent the past twenty months or so mostly isolated and come to see the presence of other humans (other than our close family or the few friends we bubbled with) as dangerous.

Back from a long day of teaching at Columbia, I take off my mask and get into a warm shower to make sure I remove all potential viruses before I hug the kids. I soap, enjoying the water, and look down at my body. Strangely, the image of my mature body gets mixed up with flitting images of my childish body. Under the hot water I go back and forth between this shower and those I took sometimes as a child. I see myself, as a child, taking a shower, and I see myself as that young child doing what I was doing then: studying my body. The doubling of the scenes is confusing. *Is this a distorted déjà vu?* I ask myself.

Once again, I feel I am chased down by a memory I never invited, and this time I cannot even tell if it is a memory or a strange projection from my present situation onto the past. The image keeps flickering despite my attempts to push it away: adult me, child me. Both taking a shower, both looking down at our bodies. I hold the soap bar tight, attempting to lock my bodily sensations in the present moment, but the image flashes back, and I see it vividly and with clear details:

> *I'm eleven or maybe twelve. I'm in the shower looking at my groin, noticing my very first pubic hairs. Then I discover I have a tiny red dot there, on the*

left side. I wonder what it is and if I should ask my mom to look and check to see if it's harmless. It's barely visible, but I note to myself that my dad has a similar red dot just like that, on the same side. Perhaps it is genetic, I think.

The vivid memory of an earlier encounter with my own naked body jolts me. *Is it a memory of an actual event? A dream? Is it a memory at all? Have I generated this now? Is this an invented memory?* I look down and confirm to myself that I do indeed have a little red mark there, a small blood dot, but I'm not sure how long I had had it or when I first noticed it. It seems like a mark of aging. I let the shower's hot water soothe my aching back. *I don't think I've always had it. I don't think I ever saw it as a child.* I try to shake this memory, which I conclude cannot be real. But the image refuses to disappear. It goes away and comes right back. I decide to make a serious effort to get rid of it using logic: *Even if I did have this dot when I was a kid, and even if I had noticed it back then, I certainly never compared it to my dad's! That simply isn't a plausible scenario.* I determine that this cannot be an actual memory. *It has to be something my brain reconstructed because I've been writing about my father and his sexuality. Yes, I invented a scenario and it floated back to me as an actual memory.*

"Come back to the present!" I command myself. *I must stop this, or I'll get trapped in this land of red dot visions.* I get out of the shower and wrap up in a big, blue towel. I try to forget about the red dot, which forces itself back so convincingly. *Ridiculous.* I would surely never have seen my father's crotch so closely. And even if I did, he was so hairy I'd never have been able to spot such a tiny dot. Still, the impact of this vision has already taken hold and I can no longer erase the idea that *we both have identical red dots*: same size, same side, same color. Knowing this might be based on a false memory doesn't shake the thought away. Eventually, I tell myself a story about it. One that I find quite convincing: Memory or not, I must at some point have noticed the red dot and used it to affirm a connectivity between my dad and me. With this interpretation, I feel calm. Comfort replaces my earlier state of alarm. *Just a little girl wanting to be like her dad: same dot, same place . . . same, same.* His body. Mine.

The Hochberg Toes

With the world slowly opening up again—kids back in school, myself back on campus, stores and restaurants opening, people walking in the streets, the city returning to itself, life coming back—the heaviness of the past two years began to lift. I realized that I'd spent way too many hours of the long closure alone in the study with his writings. Hours and hours each day for about eighteen months, just him and me. His writings and mine. His secrets, mine.

I was eager to get out, escape this memory tunnel, and live in the present. But I could no longer push him away. My dead father had become so present in my daily life that he appeared to be joining me. We walked the streets together. Him. Me. Us. At first, I was panicked. I wanted him to leave and let me be. He was dead. I was alive. But soon I realized that outside the confining borders of my study, outside in the world where life was coming back, his presence wasn't so suffocating. Even my memories were becoming lighter. Writing, as I had been, from blurred space between our bodies was unsettling, but for the first time I discovered it didn't have to be all painful or traumatic. I looked down, smiled, and shifted my attention to my toes.

If there was one thing that proved the irrefutable bond between his body and mine, it was our toes. I noticed it at a very young age, and it intrigued me greatly, given that otherwise we looked totally different. So much so that no one would ever guess I was his daughter. He had dark skin; I've always been pale. He had thick, curly, black hair; mine is light brown, thin, and straight. He had dark brown eyes; mine are green. He had a squarish body, whereas I'm narrow and slim. The fact that despite these visible differences we had such exceptionally similar toes has always been, for me, a genetic wonder. It provided me with a sense of comfort I needed as a child: It left no doubt about our chromosomal ties, despite my mother's comments about his impotency and about me being "a miracle."

I was around four or five, at the pool, when I first noticed our toe connection. First, I observed that his big toe was especially round and sizable compared to the rest of his toes, which were remarkably small. Then, I looked at my own toes and to my delight found them to be almost a mini replica of his. "You have funny toes," I told him excitedly, "and mine are the same!"

"I got mine from *savta* Tsipe," he replied with a big smile, "and you got yours from me. That is our ID card. That's how you know you are an authentic Hochberg!" We laughed and he added: "There is only one way to find out if a Hochberg is a *real* Hochberg: You have to pass the Hochberg toes test."

This must have impressed me greatly, because thirty years later, when my first child, Eli, was born, the first thing I asked Keri, after holding Eli close to my chest, was "Does he have my toes?" Her answer was unequivocally, "No." Then she laughed and said, "And that is probably a good thing."

When our second child, Omri, was born three years later, I discovered he too didn't have my toes. Neither kid passed the Hochberg test. I later observed that they have radically different toes, despite sharing the exact genetic mix. Eli's toes are small, cute, and look like little potato croquettes. Omri's toes, by contrast, are very elegant and long, more like green beans. But my interest in comparing toes, while somewhat extensive (I've mapped similarities and differences across my mother, two half brothers, and stepfather, as well), remains predominantly focused on the Hochberg lineage. And that, I concluded sadly, seemed to have come to an end.

The geography of the Hochberg toes goes like this: The big round toe contrasts sharply with the second, which curves and tilts to the right on the right foot and to the left on the left foot, as if bending down to the smaller toes to whisper a secret. It bends not drastically but slightly. More like leaning over. The tilt is visible because all the other toes face straight forward. The last three toes are significantly smaller (the pinkie is so small there's barely any room for the nail).

As a child, I was fascinated by the wrinkles of my dad's toes. These animated the toes, which, in my imagination, each had a distinct role and a developed personality. The three smallest were soldiers, like pawns on a chessboard: They followed orders. The fourth toe hovered over them like the bishop moving diagonally, making sure "those little ones were in order." The big toe was unequivocally the king: It could barely move, yet it ruled everything. The other four feared and respected it. I could spend long hours at the pool, comparing his toes to mine, which had no wrinkles but were close enough in comparison that I would imagine them growing up along similar lines.

This toe affinity, which was a source of great childhood joy, developed into a complex of sort in later years. At some point, during my late teens, I got the message (or perhaps I generated it myself) that what was perfectly fine for my dad—having funny-looking toes—was very bad news for me as a young woman. I distinctly remember the shift from a child who loved her funny toes to a teen who felt shame about them. Somehow the toes that I used to think were "cute" and "funny" had become "ugly" and "manly."

While I didn't struggle with other, more typical female body image problems, I was always busy hiding my toes and looking enviously at the feet of other women. *Why didn't I get my mom's toes?* I wondered bitterly, noting how beautiful and "feminine" hers were. Sadly, the comforting sense of the clear physical bond shared between my father and me had come to haunt me as I became indoctrinated in the unhappy ideology of gender differences and fully internalized its (arbitrary) double standards.

From the age of sixteen to almost thirty, I avoided sandals, quite a difficult task for someone who grew up in Tel Aviv weather and beach culture. I was too ashamed of my toes to expose them. And, truthfully speaking, I'm not certain I've ever fully overcome this learned complex and internalized shame, but I made a firm decision to fight it.

A few years after I moved to California for grad school, I began to walk around Berkeley in open-toed sandals. First with some hesitation, and then, when I realized no one seemed to notice, I eased into it. I concluded that in Berkeley, unlike Tel Aviv, toes, like many other items (clothes, accessories, cars, food) didn't have a gender. This was liberating on all fronts.

Now, I looked down at my toes and told myself, *I should get a nice pedicure. It has been a while.* I had been doing that since my forties, changing colors every week, loving the playfulness and the pampering. *What could be a better, more suitable gesture of love to my father*, I told myself, entertaining myself, as I walked toward the local nail spa down the street. It had been closed throughout the pandemic and had just very recently reopened. I was excited to walk in and see familiar faces. We were all hesitantly relieved. Still masked, still worried, but here. *We survived*, I thought as I smiled under my mask, glad to see Nila, glad to see that her business made it somehow. "Pick a color," Nila said. I picked light blue.

"This is for you, abba," I mumbled in Hebrew. "I choose *tekhelet*, your favorite color, like the *tekhelet* of the tzitzit." I imagined him smiling back at me and saying, "Good choice! Most befitting the royal Hochberg toes!"

Break

I took a long break. I spent six months away from anything that had to do with him, his writings, his archive, and my writing about him. It was a much-needed break.

Writers, especially academic ones, rarely share their writing process, even after their manuscripts are done. They talk about their work as if somehow it was always already there, even before it was written. As if the writing process is merely the externalization of preexisting thoughts, ideas, characters, images, words, and thoughts they carried all along in their heads. Fiction writers are much better at admitting the terror involved in the process of writing itself. The loneliness, the self-doubt, the breaks, and blocks.

I, too, as someone who has mostly published academic work, am not used to sharing my fear of writing. I learned to pretend that writing was a byproduct of other, more substantial activities, like visiting archives, "doing research," reading, mastering knowledge. But in truth, this has never been the case for me.

I never had a thought that preceded my writing. I can finally admit it openly: Writing is where thinking happens for me. Thinking, feeling, reflecting. And it always takes an experimental shape: I write, I delete, I rewrite, I think, I reflect, I write more, I rethink, I delete, etc. I cannot begin to think before I begin to write. Writing is what ignites my curiosity and slows down my mind so I can pause and have a thought. This has always been true, but with this project, it has become clear to me as never before. While I am *his* reader, *his* archivist, *his* daughter, *his* witness, the only access I have to any of these things is by writing. Writing *about* and *with* him. Writing *about* his writing. Writing *over* his writing, writing *alongside* his writing.

This writing, maybe all writing, is terrifying, and sometimes it hurts. I had to take many long breaks during this process, and these breaks too have become part of the writing. The silent months in which I took a breath away from him came with their own terror: *Will I find it in me to go back to this project? Do I really need it? Should I not just put it aside and begin a new properly academic book? Who would even care to read this? Who am I writing this for?*

Time away from writing is a time of rejuvenation but also self-doubt: *What is this book anyway? A memoir? Well, not quite. And if it is, is it his? Mine?* It is neither: not his, nor mine. If it is a memoir, it is one written between the two of us, both together and apart. All I know is that it is a work of compulsion but also love. *Is it a long love letter? Who is writing to whom?* Am I writing to him or is he writing to me, given that they are, after all, his texts I am reading and writing back to? Perhaps we are writing to each other. As is always the case between the archive and the archivist, our collaboration is my choice alone. I force it on him. I expose his writings without his consent. At this point, my earlier doubts about the merits of this work and my attempt to define it in its proper genre seem insignificant in light of the other mounting and more urgently pressing ethical concerns: Do I have the right to expose him like this? What, if anything, gives me the right to share his most secret writings (about his mental illness, his sexuality, depression, and pain) with the world? After all, he clearly didn't choose to do so. On the contrary, he had kept these writings sealed in a box, hidden in a drawer.

A break, then, was never a break. Whenever I wasn't reading him and writing about him, I was preoccupied with thoughts about it. And so, eventually, every time, after every break, no matter how long, I came back to writing. Not because I had answers or convictions. Not because I knew it was the right thing to do. I'd come back to writing because I had the feeling, irrational as it might be, that he expected me to do so: that, in his world of omens and miracles, nothing was coincidental. I had found his hidden writings, and this meant there was a reason. He, or a divine force, intended for that to happen. Now, I knew this was totally "crazy," just like I knew he wasn't the Messiah. But *he* didn't. He believed he was the Messiah, and as the chosen one (I concluded) he left me his words.

I, in turn, as his beloved daughter and loyal archivist, owed it to him to complete the task. Even if he was, as I knew he was, a false Messiah, he was my dad. His false lessons have been passed on to me, and it is my choice whether to hide them again in a sealed drawer or share them out in the open. One of us had to take the risk. *Worst-case scenario*, I tell myself, *they'll say I'm like him, crazy*. I can live with that.

My Father, the Messiah

October 14, 2022. His birthday. He would have been seventy-seven. I'm always reflective and melancholic on his birthdays. But this morning I wake up determined: "Going to delve back into his writings!" Break over.

I jump right into his later texts, the ones I'd classified as "messianic" or otherwise indicative of his extreme mood-swinging state: from frenzied to depressed. They are all organized in the blue drawer. I plan to read his stories next. Those I am perhaps most nervous to read. I am afraid they will provoke the literary critic in me. She is always ready, and she is well trained. *What if I don't like them?* I don't want to become the judge of his creative efforts. I want to hold on to the dream that he was a great writer. An undiscovered talent. A lost voice. I don't want to subject his writing to my editorial scrutiny. So for now, I put these stories aside.

I grab a few of his short notes, all written hastily, it appears, on ripped papers. The papers are scrambled with biblical quotes, to which he added his own vows:

> For you are my only God, my only judge. I am willing to do anything!
> Give thanks to *ha-Shem*, for he is good.
> Let the one who is wise not ponder the loving deeds of the one and only.

In other notes, he wrote about Moses, Aaron, Abraham, Isaac, King Samuel, and Amalek. He documented miracles and revelations and contemplated forthcoming punishments and redemptions. I try to follow the dates to see if I can trace his growing turmoil, but there are too many of these, and I become frustrated with the task.

Many of the papers are covered with stains, both pen smudges and coffee drips. Some, especially the ones that are not just a pastiche of biblical phrases, are written as lesson summaries. They open with a title and are followed with a list of items. He wrote in a prophetic tone.

The more I read of these, the clearer his emotional instability becomes to me. I am left with the nagging question: *Was he mad? Mentally ill? Or did he, like many others, simply believe in a different world order in which divine forces, revelations, and messianic messages are in control?* I have no desire or ability to answer this question, but it intensifies my sense of duty: I need to document his turmoil.

Many of these later notes are hard to read because he scribbled them and left letters unwritten. Like he had a thought but would forget it in the middle of writing. I end up spending a great deal of time guessing, decoding, tracing, recovering. *Rewriting?* I read word by word, letter by letter, making sure nothing is lost. I inscribe the present over the past: tracing his writing with mine, my pen over his pencil. Through this act, slowly and mechanically, his writing becomes mine. Like a miracle time machine, his faded words come back to life. I smile to myself thinking, *How messianic.*

I stumble upon pages and pages filled with biblical quotes and rabbinic axioms; whole chapters, copied verbatim from the Psalms, the siddur, and other Jewish sources. I am desperately looking for *his* words among these citations. Many of those are made of long-winded sentences, most of them left incomplete: passionate polemics about the limitations of rationalism, promises he made to God, stories about the glorious past and future of Jewish people. Amid all these feverish fragments, I eventually find a longer, more coherent, and fully readable paragraph:

> The world as we know it appears to us in three dimensions. But certain people, in special times, can experience more dimensions than that. Science calls this "metaphysics" and philosophers, like Immanuel Kant, give us long-winded explanations about rational principles. But Judaism gives us the only meaningful explanation for these special experiences. It is called *hitgalut* [revelation]. God never invites us to understand everything. All we are asked to do is celebrate his creation and allow *hitgalut* to come through. As it is said: *Let the one who is wise not ponder the loving deeds of the Lord.* I chose Judaism over science because it replaces the lies of rational explanations, offering instead deep belief. The only thing men have.

All of a sudden, it dawns on me: Before my dad was the Messiah, he was a professor of statistics with a worldwide reputation. And what was his area of specialty for which he gained international fame? In English it is called the "false discovery rate" (FDR). Every biostatistician knows what that means. I don't. But I am struck by the name of the field in Hebrew: *Madad ha'hitgaluyot ha'shguyot*. I repeat the Hebrew to myself out loud several times in light of my father's text. The Hebrew sounds so much more dramatic, indeed, biblical, and almost cosmic. The literal translation being "the assessment of false revelations." I wonder if I am reading too much into this, but the bitter irony of the situation cannot escape me: How appropriate that my dad, of all people, would be a visionary in the field of assessing false revelations only to later become a self-proclaimed messiah.

My Father, the Statistician

This epiphany makes me realize that until now, after five years of writing about him, I'd paid very little if any attention to his career. Or to the fact that statistics, math, calculations, predictions, and numbers were a central part of his life. His academic career bloomed and thrived for decades, long before he quit and decided he was the Messiah. I move his feverish notes aside and go back to his earlier writing.

I pull out some letters he'd written me. Among them I find a bulky, blue envelope that escaped my previous readings. It holds a short letter from him and an attached page torn out of the Northwestern University's Statistics Department's catalog of 1981. My dad had attached it and circled his name and the description with a red pen: "Professor Hochberg is visiting professor of statistics. He holds a PhD from UNC, 1974. He is one of the world's foremost contributors to the literature of the multiple comparisons problem."

Above the red circle he added a note in Hebrew: "Ask Ima to read this part to you. It will make you proud of your dad!" Did he ask me to ask my mom for help because at eleven I didn't read English well enough? Or did he want her to be aware of his achievements, too? I suspect both are true.

When I was growing up, he often told me he was "the best statistician alive" and said his findings and theories saved the world from decades of misguided scientific studies. He had the sense that the scientific world owed him massive gratitude. But at the same time, he was equally melancholic about his own professional choices. "The curse of my life," he said, when I first asked him how he became a professor of statistics. "It came easily to me, while everyone else found it so difficult, so I felt I had no choice." Statistics was something that happened to him. He never wanted it and never liked it; he simply had to do it because he was "too good at it." Even then, his "contributions to the world have not been sufficiently recognized!" He was bitter about it.

He wanted to be an actor. Or a singer. Or a playwright. Or maybe a musician. I knew he had artistic aspirations, and I knew he felt frustrated about not being creative enough. He used to talk about it openly. He took theater classes, sculpting classes, drawing classes, and eventually writing classes, but at the end he always came back to say: "Statistics is where I can be the most creative."

A tender memory flashes up before me as I place his letter back on my desk. I smile as I recall how, back in 1995, when I first told him I intended on pursuing a PhD in comparative literature, he said, "That is great, Gilly," before asking, "What does a PhD in comparative literature actually mean?" We were standing in his kitchen, and I responded theatrically, "Well, you learn how to compare books!" I demonstrated it to him, putting my left arm forward and saying, "You first hold a book in your left hand and assess it: 'This is a fine, great book.' Then," I said, pulling out my other arm, "you pick up another book in your right hand. You lift each book at a time, left, right, right, left, comparing the two before you decide which one is better!"

My dad laughed and said, "So really, it's just like statistics. All you need to do is get the variables right." Then he added, "Actually, my area in statistics is called 'multiple comparison procedures.' We have quite similar interests." With a victorious smile, he announced, "We both like to compare!"

Growing up, I knew nothing about his research. Come to think of it, I am not sure I ever even understood what statistics was. Holding the torn page from Northwestern University's catalog, I decide it is time, forty years later, for me to give it a second chance. I google his name, something I'd never done before. *Holy shit.* The man published over one hundred scientific essays! Titles like "The Distribution of the Range in General Balanced Models," "Intermediate Simultaneous Inference Procedures," and "A New Approach to Problems of Multiple Significance Testing." I learn (and feel so proud) that there is a "Hochberg formula" that is different from the Holm's method and a "Hochberg test" that is still used by biostatisticians. But I can't understand a word of it.

I print some of his publications, determined to read them, but am immediately confronted with mysterious symbols and formulas I can't read. The English words don't help much either:

One type of multiple-comparison problem involves an overall decision (conclusion, recommendation, etc.) which is based on multiple inferences. An example of this type of problem is the "multiple end points problem," which was used earlier to show that FWER control is not always needed. In this example the overall decision problem is whether to recommend a new treatment over a standard treatment. Discoveries here are rejections of null hypotheses claiming that treatment is no better than standard on specified end points. These conclusions about different aspects of the benefit of the new treatment are of interest per se, but the set of discoveries will be used to reach an overall decision regarding the new treatment. We wish therefore to make as many discoveries as possible (which will enhance a decision in favour of the new treatment), subject to control of the FDR. Control of the probability of any error is unnecessarily stringent, as a small proportion of errors will not change the overall validity of the conclusion.[35]

Terms like *multiple comparison* and *false discovery rate* recurrently appear. I feel helpless. I check out his book *Multiple Comparison Procedures* (1987) from Columbia University's library, hoping I'll be able to understand a bit more. "Error rates," "linear models," "fixed effects"—it is useless. I realize I have no chance. My father spoke and wrote in two languages I don't know: Yiddish and statistics. Both are foreign tongues I can't decipher. If I want to understand anything about his research career, I need help.

By December 2022, I give up trying to read any of his papers and decide instead to look for his book's cowriter, Professor Ajit C. Tamhane. He is easy to find. A South Asian man in his late seventies, he is teaching at Northwestern University, where I send him an email. He responds immediately to my request to meet on Zoom and seems genuinely happy to do so.

A few days later, we meet on screen. His warm smile and soft voice put me at ease. He looks younger than expected and is talkative and alert.

"Your dad and I met when he was a graduate student. I was already an assistant professor back then, and he was so driven and charismatic, it was clear he was a rising star. At twenty-eight he was already publishing essays. So I was happy when he suggested we work together."

Ajit talks fondly about my dad, and this makes me feel less lonely. He shares memories freely and seems to enjoy it.

"So, your dad called me, I think by then he might have already been at Indiana University, I'm not sure, but I remember his call very well. He said: 'I'm good with coming up with ideas, but I have no patience to write them down or develop them, so I suggest that we work together—I'll send you the ideas, and you work on developing them. We'll make a good team.'"

"Did the plan work?" I ask.

"Well, we managed to publish the book, and you may not know this, but the book was a game changer. It's still used. It reshaped the field."

"I know nothing about your field," I say. "Strange how little my dad told me about his work."

"He was brilliant, really," Ajit continues. "He popped out ideas every second. But once he had an idea, he lost interest. That's why he needed me. My job was to turn those ideas into chapters."

We both laugh.

Ajit continues: "Your dad would send me massive drafts by mail, there was no email back then. *Massive*. I kept telling him, 'Yossi, slow down.' But there was no slowing down with him. That was how he worked. Ideas kept pouring out of him. Piles of paper kept coming my way. That's how we worked. He would send ideas and half-baked papers, and my job was to make sense of them. He provided the spark; I provided the structure. We worked well together. Even if sometimes he drove me crazy."

The last word Ajit utters allows me to finally dare to ask, "And how was it later? Did you continue to work together? I mean, after he got sick?"

Ajit appears less enthusiastic to talk about this. Eventually, after a few seconds of uncomfortable silence, he responds politely, "Your father was brilliant but very intense. And he got even more intense in later years. So, we stopped working closely. But we met in 1995. I will say... he was different by then."

"How different?" I push, despite noticing that Ajit was no longer enjoying this conversation.

Restless in his chair, he finally says: "Well, I can share an anecdote.... We met at Tel Aviv University at a large international conference your father organized. He seemed fine during the first session. Then, he invited me and a few other colleagues for a ride around Tel Aviv. He wanted to show us the city. Once we got into his car, he turned to us and whispered, 'You should crouch down when we're driving. The Hamas know my number plate and they're after me. They know I'm the secret leader of the Jewish people... the Messiah, so they're trying to get rid of me.'"

Ajit looks serious and says hesitantly: "So... yes... I guess you could say that Yossi changed a lot from the time I first met him. He also changed politically. Back in the late 1970s and then during the 1980s when we worked together, he was outspoken and critical of Israel. Then in 1995, he lectured all the guests at the conference about the importance of Zionism, the biblical promise of the land, Palestinian terrorists, and the arrival of the Messiah. We *all* knew something was wrong."

"Yes, I know," I respond. "His illness developed in that way. Maybe because all forms of national chauvinism are madness. He joined the crowd."

Ajit is more comfortable now that he realizes I am not offended by his critique of my father. He volunteers more: "I met him again, for the last time, in 2001 in Philadelphia. But by then he was really not well. I mean, really *not well*. He was invited to give some talks at Temple University, but he was confused and incoherent. He began talking, but his words were scattered, delusional. He kept showing the statistical proof of the existence of God. It was sad. Eventually someone had to get him off the platform."

How humiliating this must have been for him, I think, and I feel deep sorrow.

"He was a giant. A real star," Ajit concludes. "Such a loss."

The conversation with Ajit saddens me, but it also empowers me. I am not the only one who lost him and not the only one who senses he once was "a real star." I wait a few more days before I contact another of his former colleagues; one I know from childhood — the Israeli statistician Yoav Benjamini, who, back in 2014, just a few months after my father died, won the National Israeli Science Award for research he'd begun working on with my dad in the 1990s. I'd spoken to Yoav soon after my father's shivah. He called me to share his award speech and the PowerPoint presentation he'd made, which included photos of my dad and quotes from their collaborative work. Now, after the call with Ajit, I want to hear more, and Yoav is happy to talk.

"Your father was the reason why I got into working in this area of 'false discovery rate,'" Yoav tells me on Zoom. "I had no intention of getting involved in what seemed to be, back in the late 1980s, a totally marginal subfield."

This is my opportunity to finally get a sense of what the hell *false discovery rate* meant, so I ask. "Well," Yoav continues, after clearing his throat, "it is the *ratio* of the number of false positive results to the number of total positive test results." I pretend to understand. "*False discovery rate* translates in Hebrew into: *Madad ha'hitgaluyot ha'shguyot*," Yoav adds.

"Yes, I know," I tell him, as I wonder if he too sees the bitter irony of the situation. The man who studied "false revelations" in time became a self-nominated Messiah.

Yoav proposes an explanation of the Benjamini–Hochberg collaboration, "the basis for his long-lasting research." He shares his screen, talking me through it. The method can be performed as follows:

To control fdr ≤ α:

1. Let p(1) ≤ ⋯ ≤ p(M) be ordered p-values.
2. Define L = max j: p(j) < αj/M.
3. Reject all hypotheses Hoj for which pj ≤ p(L).

But I can't decipher the formulas or follow his words. Eventually he gives up on me understanding statistics and sums up: "You know, Yossi was always worried about science. That is why he was interested in *false discovery*. He once told me that the problem wasn't that scientists might fail to get the right findings but that we're more likely to get findings wrong and still think they're right. For him, the real danger of science was that people believed in it too much."

Yoav's words stick with me because they give a certain coherence to my father, who otherwise seemed totally fragmented. A "once-great scientist" who one day suddenly became a "mad, false Messiah." Listening to Yoav helps me realize that my two dads, "the statistician" and "the crazed devotee," were one person all along. The man who published academic scientific essays was the same man who suspected science and believed in miracles and divine intervention. Indeed, *as a scientist*, he devoted his time to demonstrating the limitations of scientific findings. It is this same suspicion in science that I now saw clearly running throughout *all* of his writings—academic and personal, before and after his mental breakdown. Somehow, finding this coherence and uniting my "two dads" gives me some sense of comfort.

"Your father was a giant," Yoav tells me at the end of our Zoom conversation. "He was a real groundbreaker. In the field of statistics one could even say he was indeed a Messiah!" We exchange a sad smile of resignation before we hang up.

On my desk, in my small study at home, I've always kept a photo of my dad standing by a bookshelf in a university office. He is in his mid-thirties. His back to the camera, his face turned toward us, smiling. He's wearing brown corduroy pants and a white sweater. He looks youthful and handsome. I stare at the picture and try to reimagine him as the energized professor he used to be. The man I remember from my childhood. The dad I visited each summer, each time in a different city, different campus. I stare at the picture and remind myself that he wasn't always sick, mad, delusional, depressed, puffy, absent, lost. He was a successful professor. He was full of life. He was funny and good-looking. And

Dad in his office. Bloomington, Indiana, 1980.

I was his proud daughter. My eyes begin to tear. I look longer at the image and study his body language: small shoulders, his neck twisted, who is he smiling at? His left hand is reaching out for a book on the shelf. I look so closely that I begin to feel that I can smell his office. The longer I stare at the photo, the more animated he becomes. *Yes! This is the father I remember! The one I want to remember the most.* I continue to look deep into the frame. And for a second I am convinced that it is me he is looking back at, so I lift the photo, bring it closer to my face, and smile back.

January 2023

New York

Beyond Interpretation

January 1st. A new year. Almost ten years had passed since his death and over five since I began this writing experiment. By now, I had read so many of his texts and visited him as a dad, a letter writer, a statistician, a Messiah, a madman, a sad man, a lonely man, a sexual being. I finally felt ready to read his prose. He had made a clear distinction between texts he considered worthy for their "literary value" and others he considered personal musings or political manifestoes. While all his texts are handwritten, the ones he considered "literary" he typed and headed: "STORY."

He had written these typed-up stories between 1982 and 1985, when he was enrolled in creative writing classes at NYU. I remembered him telling me about them and about "finding his real vocation in fiction writing." Unlike everything else, his prose is well-organized, stapled, and preserved: "Little Red Riding Hood" by Yosef Hochberg; "Going Out" by Yosef Hochberg; "Ali's Dream" by Yosef Hochberg; "Relationships" by Yosef Hochberg; "Divorce" by Yosef Hochberg; "The Case of a Capricious Pen" by Yosef Hochberg.

He clearly took this seriously and wrote these stories with the intention of sharing with others, perhaps publishing. He used Wite-Out to cover mistakes and a red pen to add revision notes on the side, perhaps based on peer review ("Remember to add a longer description of the woman," "Make sure this section is in the right place," "Develop his character or take him out").

Of all the stories I found, only one was written in Hebrew. On the top of the first page he handwrote in English: "Send out for translation." Did he? Did he ever send any of his stories out for publication? Did he try? Were they rejected? I hope not. I don't want to feel retroactive disappointment and humiliation on his behalf. I know too well how bad it feels to send something out and get rejected. I've experienced it many times, and I have no desire to put him through this. Not even now, when he is already dead.

Reading, writing, writing about writing. That is what I do for a living. I feast on other people's writings. But these past years, I've learned that his writings are different. I am not sure I know how to read or write about them. His writings are not like anything else I have ever seen before. After years of reading Martin Heidegger, Jacques Derrida, Jacques Lacan, Roland Barthes, I thought I knew how to read beyond clear interpretation. But I have come to see that these men, allegedly daring to write after the subject, have all written from a very safe and coherent place. Their mastery of subjectivity is what enabled them to write so lavishly about nonbeing, fragmentation of the Ego, the illusion of subjectivity, or the death of the author. My father's writings are not like that. They are not philosophical or linguistic exercises about the dissolution of the self. Nor are they romanticized depictions of creative madness, depression, and abjectness, as we find in Julia Kristeva or Georges Bataille. There is nothing sublime, romantic, abstract, or metaphysical about my father's writings. He does not write *about* the end of subjectivity, depression, or abjectness. He writes *from within* the highs of delusion and the lows of abjection. Such texts do not invite interpretive engagement. They resist and block the critic from analyzing. To me they say, "Read!" and nothing else. So, I read. The Quran also opens with the command "Iqra!" (read/recite). *What else is there to do?*

I learned to read him and do my best to resist my compulsion for interpretation. Instead, I tried to swallow his words, the verbal manifestations of his troubled mind. His language is something I could never replicate. His writing is free of sublimation. It comes from the other side: abject and manic. His writing cries. His world, made of biblical figures, miracles, coded messages, revelations, punitive consequences—but also cum and hemorrhoids—comes to life like a wild beast with a yamuka. *What do his stories read like?* I wonder, the texts he structured and codified "literary."

If I'm going to read these, I must read them without *my literary critic hat on*, I promised myself. And I did. I read them, one by one. It took a full week to do so. Candidly speaking, I don't think they are any good. It saddens me greatly. His poems aren't great either. I was sad, but even more so, I felt ashamed of myself for judging his writing so harshly. Deep inside, I had to admit that my disappointment was grave. I was hoping to discover a Jewish Anton Chekhov. Alas, my father was not.

However, one story, "Havilot" (Packages), the only one written in Hebrew, opened a whole world for me. It too is by no means a great story, but reading it reminded me that my dad wasn't just my dad. He was a son, a brother, a cousin. It ignited my curiosity. It made me want to get to know the person he was before he became my dad. I wanted to meet the child he once was and the young man he became long before I came along.

National Amnesia, Forced Forgetting

"Havilot" is typed in small, faded, squarish Hebrew letters on a white square of paper with small holes on both sides of the page. A familiar sight. I smile, summoning a vivid memory of the unforgettable screechy sound of the dot matrix printer: *eeeeee, gzzzzzzz, eeeeeeee, gzzzzzzzz*. I continue to hear it buzzing in my ears as I read his Hebrew text, already translating it in my head to English:

> My mom and her sister Bluma used to meet every day with their husbands and their kids. They would gather in our small, dark living room in Yahud, dressed in heavy winter clothes, even in the summer. Normally they spoke Yiddish and included us kids in conversations and stories, but they switched to Polish or Russian when they wanted to make sure we couldn't understand.

I had no idea that my grandparents spoke Polish, let alone Russian. I knew they both grew up in small, impoverished shtetl in Poland, but given that they had so little formal education, I assumed they knew only very basic Polish, no more than they needed for simple communication with Poles. My grandmother had never indicated she knew Polish. In fact, she made an effort to explain that she wasn't even a Pole. "There is no such thing as Polish Jews," she declared in anger when I asked her to renew her Polish citizenship so that I could have access to a European passport. She didn't like that request, to say the least: "At lo mitbayeshet? Darkon Polani? Ma eetakh?" (Do you have no shame? A Polish passport? Are you out of your mind?)

Like many so-called third-generation Israelis, I was delighted when I found out that, if I could secure a Polish passport, I could finally become the European Jew my grandparents never were: cosmopolitan, modern, secular, almost a "real European." I wanted to get out of Israel, which for me was a prison. A place of war, conflict, violence. I had no idea my request would upset my grandmother. Nor did I know she was capable of being so expressive. But Tsipe was angry, and she made her anger known. When I apologized and said, "It's just a practical matter. It would allow me to get work in Europe," she fired back, "Polin zeh lo inyan prakti!" (Poland is not a practical matter!) I never again brought up the subject.

Still, my dad writes that they spoke both Polish and Russian. It always amazes me how necessity makes language acquisition easy, or at least doable. Languages that people otherwise spend long years studying are picked up in very short periods by refugees and others who need these languages to survive. Neither of

My father (at almost two years old) and extended family. Displaced persons camp, Germany, 1947. Dad is seated in the middle on his grandmother Leah's lap (she would die two years later). To their sides, his parents: Hirschel and Tsipe. Behind them, from *right to left*: Tsipe's brother Shalom and his wife, Ida; Tsipe's brother Duvid and his wife, Fruma; and Tsipe's young brother-in-law, Itzhak, with his wife, Bluma. Both sisters, Tsipe and Bluma, are pregnant. In 1949, Leah and her adult children Tsipe, Bluma, and Duvid, along with all of their children, would be sent to live in the newly established state of Israel and settled in Yahud. Shalom and his wife moved to New York City, thanks to her American citizenship.

my grandparents finished middle school, yet they each spoke four and a half languages: Yiddish, Polish, Russian, some German, and Hebrew. The last they were forced to learn later in life in order to be able to communicate with their grandchildren who grew up in a state that enforced linguistic and cultural amnesia on its citizens.

Jews born in Israel, like me, grow up thinking that we have no past, only a present. Israel was built through a carefully guarded regime of erasure. Palestinians and their past have been erased, of course, but also anything that could have challenged the unity of the newly created Jewish nation had to be forcefully forgotten. And so, my grandparents' world was and forever remains mostly unknown and sealed to me. They learned not to speak about it, and when I asked, I would always get the same response: "Ma sh-haya haya. Zeh lo chashuv" (Whatever happened, happened, and it's not important).

My dad didn't like to talk about their past, either. He wanted only to talk about his own greatness as the "smartest, toughest, strongest, bravest" kid in Yahud. I grew up with a very limited sense of my family's history. As a child, I simply concluded that there was none. My mother's family, originally from Russia, settled in Palestine in the late 1800s as socialists with a Zionist agenda. But I knew very little about them either. Whenever I asked my mother about them, she responded, "I really don't know anything. They never talked about this." Nor did she seem eager to ever find out. This was not a unique situation. I grew up like most Israeli Jews with a chaotic present, about which we knew very little, and no past.

My generation was born into a young nation that, we were told, "came about miraculously" or through "divine intervention." Every Israeli Jewish child learns from day one that they are part of "the redemption": *Me-shoa le-tekuma* (from Shoah to Rebirth). *Tekuma ve-gevora* (Rebirth and heroism). That is all there is. No questions asked. No answers given. My father's parents' past of fear and hardship was made foreign, hidden, despicable. Their memories, their suffering, their loss, their language had no place in this new nation, where Hebrew alone was to be spoken and the rich Jewish diasporic world was to be forgotten.

Like most Israeli Jews, I know only a few words in Yiddish. The language my father dreamed in. The language of my grandparents, their parents, and that of most Eastern European Jews, those who survived the Nazi genocide and those who did not. *What a crime*, I think to myself. *What violence, erasure, forced forgetting.*

I pick up my father's text again, feeling it is not just about me connecting to him. No. This has now become about my commitment to a much larger picture. My commitment to my family's memory. My commitment to bear witness. To re-remember and pass on *their story. Mine.* The story of the past that was kept away from me by state violence. Fueled with this sense of injustice and need for historical reclamation, I read on. His story gives me access to a snapshot of a past otherwise unknown and inaccessible to me.

One scene in particular grabs my attention. It is beautifully written and animated. The scene describes my grandmother and her younger sister getting together for their weekly weekend family reunion in Yahud:

Both sisters had the exact same furniture, same dishes, same curtains, and the same photograph of their eldest brother, Dov, who died during the war, hung on the central wall in the living room. You couldn't tell in which house you were, because they were identical. The two sisters also looked alike and dressed alike, but their facial expressions told them apart: My mother's eyes were always sad and she rarely smiled. Bluma, on the other hand, had a cheerful expression and positive outlook.

Every Shabbat, we would all gather together in one of the apartments. But once in six months or so there was a big celebration. And we, all kids, waited for it eagerly: our uncle, Shalom, whom we have never met, and who was the only sibling to not come to Yahud but rather move from Germany to the United States, after marrying an American Jewish woman, would send a package! On the day the package arrived, all of us — Bluma, my mom, Duvid, their younger brother, Haim, myself, and our four cousins — would gather together to open it and split the goods. We kids would attack the well-wrapped box with our little hands and teeth, making our parents laugh. Finally, we would pull out extra-large men's buttoned shirts, long, wide pants, funny hats, and strange underwear. *Everything was huge. Always.* We would grab the large fabrics and run with the new outfits to prepare a show. It became our anticipated family dress-up party. *Large underwear over the head, long pants dragging on the floor, shirts that fit like long nightgowns.* We played with these massive clothes for hours, while the adults sat in the living room and whispered to each other in Yiddish: "What are these *shmattes*? Why does he continue to send us these ugly scraps? Is this what folks wear in America?!"

At this point I am reading and laughing out loud, imagining my father and his brother and cousins dressing up in the *shmattes* their uncle sent from America. My father's cousins, whom I'd seen only occasionally growing up, are nevertheless central to me, and remain so despite the fact that I see them and their families once in a decade at most. They somehow continue to hold for me a tie to a past: a history, a tradition, and a memory to which I otherwise have no access. I imagine the six kids—my dad; Haim, his brother; Leah and Batia, Bluma's daughters; and Yossi and Benni, the sons of Duvid's sons—dressing up in the extra-large *shmattes* their uncle sent from New York City, because those were likely the only clothes he could afford. I am filled with tenderness toward these people whom I hardly know but who surely knew my father much better than I ever did.

Tsipe and Hirschel Hochberg

I grew up feeling embarrassed about my father's parents, wishing they were more modern, more educated, more assimilated. Visiting them felt like entering a time machine. Their apartment was always dark and cold. They never turned on the lights ("no need") or the heat ("too expensive") and the shades were always down ("better not to be seen"). They looked and behaved as if time had stood still: They were still living in a shtetl, attached to old rituals, and wearing clothes from another era and another climate. I hated the smell of their old wool sweaters, which they wore throughout the hot summers. They were foreign implants in a place that never became their home.

My grandfather, Hirschel, used to pace around the apartment singing in Yiddish, while Tsipe would mumble, turning to us grandchildren, saying in broken Hebrew, "Lo shotek ha-tipesh hazeh!" (Never shuts up, this idiot!). It wasn't hard to tell that my grandmother disliked my grandfather. She made no secret of it. I felt sorry for him for how badly she treated him, but I also felt sorry for her. Her soft, watery, grayish eyes and faint smile made her look so sad and defeated. Her pain was too heavy for me to bear. I could see, even as a very young kid, that she never got to live and that her entire life was about nothing but surviving.

Tsipe and Hirschel met in 1943 in a labor camp in Kazakhstan. She arrived from Krasnobród, a small Jewish town near Lublin in East Poland, accompanied by her mother, two younger brothers, and younger sister. He, an escapee from Bialystok, West Germany, was the only one from his family to survive the Nazi invasion. They both made their way first to Russia, then to Siberia, where they were treated as Polish prisoners of war, from there to Uzbekistan, before finally settling in Jambyl, Kazakhstan, where my father would be born a year later.

Growing up, I heard very little about these difficult years and the ones that followed: their failed return to Poland, their escape to Czechoslovakia, then to

Yosale with his parents. Zhambyl, Kazakhstan (my dad's birthplace), late 1945 or early 1946.

Austria, and finally to Germany, where they settled in a displaced persons camp from 1946 to 1949 and where Haim, their younger son, was born. Like many Jewish refugees from Poland, they naively waited for the war to end, thinking they would be able to go back to their hometowns. Little did they know that the Poles had no intention of ever welcoming them back. Upon returning to Krasnobród, they discovered that none of their Jewish neighbors or extended family had survived and that the Poles who took over their homes and whatever remained of their property had no intention of surrendering it back. "To think that we refused to accept Russian citizenship because we were holding on to our Polish one," Tsipe would complain. "Turns out that for the Poles, Jews were never Polish."

The other thing I did know, because Tsipe would not miss an opportunity to remind us grandchildren, was that "in Jambyl they were finally safe." They worked hard and had little to eat, but "unlike the Russians and the Poles, the Kazakhstanis made us feel human again."

Eventually, in early 1949, Hirschel, Tsipe, and their two sons, along with Tsipe's younger sister Bluma and her two daughters and her brother Duvid and his two sons, boarded a boat from Germany to Palestine, which by then had become the newly established Jewish State, Israel. They joined hundreds of thousands of Jewish war refugees, which Europe was eager to send away (a dark, cruel "solution" to the so-called Jewish Problem), and thus they found themselves in a place they knew by name from prayers but had no aspirations to inhabit.

In fourth grade, I had a school assignment (it was probably nationwide): "Interview your older relatives and write down their stories of survival. If they are Holocaust survivors, write details about their experience and how they were saved and brought to Israel." I knew my grandparents on my mother's side lived in Palestine since the late nineteenth century, so they didn't count. My father's parents were survivors, but they managed to escape in time to Siberia, thus avoiding Nazi concentration camps. I remember feeling slightly upset by that. I knew they suffered on the run and that they worked hard and were treated badly by the Soviets, and I figured that was at least "second best." I was eager to interview them and hear all about their misery *there* and their rebirth *here*.

I thought nothing of this assignment. It made perfect sense. We were told time and time again that we were a young nation of survivors. *We were all survivors.* Even if your family didn't suffer directly at the hands of the Nazis, they suffered. The important lesson, and the one we were all indoctrinated into, was that everyone—whether your family came from Poland, Germany, France, Morocco, Egypt, or even right here in Palestine—was "a people in recovery." The motto "Me-shoa le-tekuma" united us all, even if the subtext was that some of us were a little more entitled to this honorary status than others.

The following week, we gathered, the three of us, Tsipe, Hirschel, and me, for the interview in their small apartment in Petach Tikvah. We sat around the narrow Formica table in the kitchen drinking chilled Tempo Cola (the Israeli mimic of Coca-Cola). He seemed jumpy and eager, she significantly less so.

I opened my notebook and read out my question: "How was it during the war? Please tell me *ALL* about your suffering and relatives who died and then how you came here."

Hirschel jumped right in. "Siberia was the worst. We had nothing. I worked cutting logs all day and all night. We had nothing to eat and we were cold all the time. It was much better in the displaced persons camp. We were there for a few years. It was much better. Much better. The Germans gave us clothes, and food, and..."

"Idiot!" Tsipe hissed. "Shut up!" She silenced him and then added, "He understands nothing. Idiot. It was terrible. All of it: Terrible in Poland, terrible in Siberia, terrible everywhere. We had nothing. We were hungry. We weren't human. Terrible."

"But you wanted to come to Israel, and they got you here so now you are happy, right?" I asked eagerly, hoping to score a great answer on the positive end of things.

"Eizo She'ela zo bikhlal?" (What kind of a question is that?), she responded, impatiently. She continued: "What does 'wanting' have to do with any of this?! No one wanted us to stay, we *had* to go. And besides, it was an arrangement. *Everything those days was an arrangement*: Going to Russia was an arrangement, going back to Germany was an arrangement. Israel too was an arrangement. Coming here was an arrangement. Even my marriage was an arrangement! This had nothing to do with us wanting anything. We stopped wanting a long time ago. We were told to get on the boat, so we got on the boat!"

I thanked them both for the interview, but I knew that this surely was not what the teacher expected. I told myself I would have to make a few changes, reassuring myself that Tsipe's harsh words were not true. *She surely didn't mean that. Of course they wanted to come here to rebuild and rebirth! I'll just have to change that part.*

As for her snarky comment about her marriage, that didn't surprise me. I was used to her bashing him. We all were. And it wasn't just her. My father, Haim, and even Tsipe's siblings were always dismissive of him.

"Such a clown."

"Don't listen to him. He has no idea what he's talking about."

"When will he stop with his silly jokes."

As grandchildren, Udi, Danny, and I knew the hierarchy was clear: Tsipe was revered and loved by her sons; Hirschel was tolerated despite no one in the family respecting him.

As a child, I never asked myself why Tsipe would marry a man she and her family so clearly looked down on. But in future years, long after my father died, Haim would share his theory with me. And whether it was true or not, it made perfect sense. It also made for a great story.

January 2018
Tel Aviv

Kazakhstani Lover

I hadn't met Haim for five years. Not since we last met at my father's grave. I was surprised and moved when I got a call from him in New York. He said he was sorry he hadn't kept in touch and expressed his desire to meet and "build a relationship." We decided to meet in January, while I visited Israel.

Growing up, I wasn't close to Haim and rarely met up with his family. My father and Haim had a tense and competitive relationship to begin with, and after my father remarried and Haim divorced, they grew even further apart. Beyond sibling rivalry, there was the open secret known to the entire family: My father was their mother's favorite son. Everyone knew it; my grandmother never tried to hide it. This meant that every opportunity Haim had to tease my father, he did.

As a child, I'd watch him perform the same stand-up comedy routine nearly every time the extended family got together: "Notice how Yossi looks different from all the rest of us?" he would ask, addressing the four cousins. We all knew what would follow and would laugh in concert. "Notice that *all* the men in our family have the same body frame—tall, slim, narrow, strong—and *all* of us have fair skin and green eyes. ALL but Yossi: He is short, bulky, and has brown eyes. He is hairy and he is dark. *Where did he come from?*"

At this point, Benny or another cousin would usually add some funny stories about my dad's youth and mention humorously that "he is also the only one in the family with brains!"

Haim and my father didn't just look very different; everything they did, and all the choices they made, were poles apart: My father was always the studious one, first attending an elite yeshiva, then college, then graduate school, finally

Tsipe, Haim (Dad's younger brother), Dad, and Hirschel. The yellow star sticker added to the album reads: "Haim Is Born! Germany, 1948."

becoming a professor. Haim thought very little of formal education, quit high school midway, and started working with diamonds, slowly but surely becoming an independent and very successful businessman. As my dad aged, he grew moodier and implosive, while Haim developed an air of calmness. My father became ill, mentally and physically, while Haim became the epitome of health. He ate well, exercised daily, and practiced yoga to align his body and soul. I often wished my father were more like his brother: calm, strong, reassuring, alive.

We met at a small café in central Tel Aviv during my short visit in January 2018.

I recognized his slim silhouette as he came through the door. Almost seventy years old, he looked much younger. Fit, tall, a big smile on his face.

"Hi, Gilly," he said with his distinctively soft voice. As I melted into his slow, measured, soothing voice, I was reminded of my father's frantic, manic episodes and his final puffy body on the hospital bed. Unlike him, Haim was able to escape their tragic upbringing: the mark of the war, the trauma of their refugee parents, the legacy of the Holocaust, the shtetl mentality of the family, the poverty they grew up with, the small-town borders of Yahud, the town they grew up in, their parents' fear and isolation. Unlike my dad, Haim, the successful businessman, walked the walk, leaving his family's religious, exilic mentality behind. My dad too tried to escape, but he always found his way back: back to the shtetl, to religion, to trauma, and, above all, to his mother. Those two were glued together.

Haim ordered coffee and smiled. He began the meeting by telling me he was sorry. "I should have kept in touch after his death." His green eyes got watery.

"I'm glad we are finally meeting," I said.

Haim leaned back, took a sip of his coffee, and said with a sad smile, "The only person able to lighten Tsipe's face was your father. With him, she relaxed and softened. Her only joy in life was Yossi; 'Yossi this, Yossi that, Yossi, Yossi, Yossi.' She loved him more than anyone. Anything. He was her life."

It was no secret that he was her chosen son or, as Haim put it, "her man." The two of them had a close and special bond. When they talked (always in Yiddish), the rest of the world disappeared. They melded into each other, leaving the rest of us outside their sacred bond. Hirschel, on his end, was fully ignored by my dad, by Haim, by everyone in the family. The explanation I had for this, and it wasn't hidden, was that she was forced into marriage during the war and never loved him. She didn't even *like* him.

Growing up I was told, first by my dad, then by Haim, and finally by my grandmother herself, that "Hirschel was a small man, with small aspirations, with little interest in anything but himself." The modus operandi was to ignore him, as he seemed to ignore all of us. He was simply there, pacing around, often singing to himself in Yiddish.

"Why did she marry a man she loathed? What were the circumstances of this alleged forced marriage?" I asked my dad as I grew older, only to learn that "it was war time and the family did what they thought was best for the family." I had no idea that this was the main reason Haim arranged our meeting, the first in five years. The first of just the two of us, ever.

Haim took another sip of his coffee and then said in his distinctly slow, measured way, stretching the words so that I was ready to lean into whatever it was that he was about to say, "Gilly, there is one thing I wanted to tell you after Yossi died, and I'm sorry it took me too long to do so."

He is going to talk about how my dad left me out of his will and how shameful it was and how he, my uncle, should have said something, done something about it, I was thinking even before we met. *He is going to do the right thing, as my father's wealthy brother... He is going to tell me that* HE *will add me to his will*. I was fairly convinced this was the purpose of the meeting.

So I was both utterly shocked and disappointed when Haim said, "Let's just jump right into it, no point in going in circles. Are you ready for a shocker?" He winked.

"Ready as can be," I answered with a grin.

"Okay, here we go then. What I'm going to tell you now is kind of a family secret, but really everyone knows it, we all always knew it, although we all pretend not to. You see... Hirschel, my father, your grandfather, wasn't your father's biological father."

My grandfather was not my father's father? This I surely didn't expect. I froze and just continued to stare at Haim. *What does this even mean...*

Haim allowed for the confusion and surprise to pass before he continued, "I don't have a clear, definite proof of this, but there are good reasons to suspect this is true, and there is a very reasonable theory behind this." He snuck a quick gaze toward me to see my reaction, and once he felt I was ready he went on. "For one, Tsipe arrived in Jambyl at least a year before she met Hirschel and, when you consider the dates, and the time of her pregnancy, you realize it doesn't align. I calculated this. She must have been pregnant *before* she met my dad."

I finally gathered my voice and asked, "So who is my dad's dad?"

Haim was prepared. "Well, it is hard to say for sure. *But*, based on my research, our mother's hints, and your father's distinct and very different looks, I think it is safe to conclude that his biological father was a local Kazakhstani man. Maybe her employer at the labor camp? Maybe a lover? I hope it wasn't forced on her."

After this deluge, Haim stopped talking for a while and we both sat looking around quietly. Then he went on. "Based on my research, our mother must have been forced to marry Hirschel, for the sake of her younger siblings, their reputation. She had to cover up the shame. Pregnant out of marriage, and from a non-Jew, even worse."

"Do we know this for sure?"

"We'll never know for sure because they are all dead, but I think it is safe to assume it is. I visited the town and I asked around and I've done lots of research and... there is your father's distinct looks, you know... and... she loved him differently. I think it is safe to assume that his father was not Hirschel. He was a Kazakhstani. And I also know he wasn't Jewish. He was most likely Muslim. And guess what?" Haim's voice sounded excited for the first time. "I know this because of your father's genetic back disease! I researched some. It is not a Jewish Ashkenazi disease, his muscle condition, it is common among some eastern Europeans and mostly Muslims! And he was the only one in the entire family that had it. So there, surely different DNA."

This was big news, and very different from the news I expected to receive. I was trying to come back to my body, and he was waiting for me to adjust to this news before going on.

"It's good news for you, from a medical perspective. This means you are a quarter Muslim Kazakhstani. It means your blood is mixed. You're not just Jewish Ashkenazi. It is much better for your health! Mixed blood reduces many genetic diseases, all that inbreeding, you know."

Haim always thought about health. Still, his upbeat tone took me by surprise. He seemed relieved, even comforted by the fact that he and my dad didn't share the same father. *Was it because my father was so ill, mentally and physically?* I think to myself and conclude that, yes, this surely offered Haim a sense that my father's illnesses of mind and body were fully separated from him and that his own health and mental composition were safe. "Different DNA!" But then I realized there must be more to it. This different father likely also provided him with a reasonable answer to what must have been a painful experience throughout his life: Tsipe's clear preference of my dad over him. Before I even had a chance to think about what I was going to say, my words came out: "At least now we know why she was so close to abba, or why, as you said, she 'was all about Yossi, Yossi, Yossi.' I mean, who could possibly compete with a son of a Kazakhstani lover?"

"Exactly," Haim said, laughing. "Surely no one who is Hirschel's son!"

Several months later, Haim suggested I take a DNA test to confirm his Kazakhstani hypothesis. I was initially inclined to but eventually decided against it. I liked Haim's theory, whether realistic or speculative. The truth was, I didn't want it proven wrong. It made for a good story. What do I care if the one-quarter Kazakhstani is found in my DNA or not? I want to stay with the belief that my grandmother, the woman I knew as hardworking, sad, and bitter, was once happier, perhaps even in love with a Kazakhstani man. I have no desire or motivation to prove otherwise.

Haim too was invested in this narrative for his own reasons. When I told him I decided not to seek "scientific verification," he agreed and added that "those DNA tests are *at best* 50 percent accurate.... We won't learn anything definite from it anyway." Together, we decided the story made perfect sense and explained otherwise unanswered questions: my father's different looks, rare genetic disease, his mental illness. We need no further proof, the two of us concluded. "That must have been what differentiated him from the rest of the family," Haim added. "There is no way a brain like his came from *my* dad."

"No doubt," Haim and I concluded: "A Kazakhstani lover. It explains EVERYTHING."

April 2023

Petach Tikvah

The Cousins

Five years had passed since I began archiving my father and spending so much time alone with his writings. I was beginning to feel lonely. The long pandemic years, the isolation, the fact that my father, my cowriter, was dead made my need for company intensify. Above all, I began to feel the pressing need to share the burden of memory. It was time for me to reconnect with the only living people I knew, other than Haim, who cared about him almost as much as I did: his four cousins. They grew up together, they knew him as the child, the teen, and the young man he was long before I came into this world.

I wrote to Haim, telling him I'd be visiting Israel in April and asked if he would be willing to gather the cousins. I hadn't seen my father's four cousins since the shivah and, frankly, had no idea if they had any time or interest in meeting. "They would love to see you," Haim reassured me. "Everyone is excited," he reported back after calling. "We never get together. Thanks to you, we finally will!"

The cousins. My dad, the oldest, is in the center, his brother Haim to the right, and cousin Benny on the left; Batia is between them, and Leah is in the stroller. Yahud, 1951.

My father's four cousins—Leah, Batia, Yossi, and Benny—always admired him. During my childhood, whenever my father visited Israel, he would take me to see his uncle Duvid, who lived in Yahud, and his aunt Bluma, who lived in Petach Tikvah. I loved those visits. The cousins and their many kids would always be there, and conversations would quickly turn to the past and almost always center on my dad. Duvid, my grandmother's youngest sibling, would light a small fire in the backyard and we would sit around it for hours, the cousins sharing memories about their childhood, when they all lived nearby in the same small neighborhood in Yahud. The stories were the same year after year, but each time we enjoyed them anew:

"Remember the time Yossi broke into the synagogue? Hahahaha!"

"Your father was such a wild one!"

"And the biblical contests he used to run? Asking questions only he knew the answers to?"

"He would offer prizes to the winners and then collect them himself, plus the money from the tickets. Hahaha."

"He was shrewd, your dad, always smarter than all of us put together."

My father, for his part, would mostly listen, drinking in the praise, looking at me to make sure I too was proud of him. I was. Unlike the rest of them, he escaped the shtetl, which was the only reality they and their parents knew. Duvid, his wife, Fruma, and their sons, Yossi and Benny, were no longer religious, but they were never far from their small-town mentality. Bluma and her daughters, Batia and Leah, became ultrareligious, much more so than my grandparents, and joined the Zionist religious movement as enthusiasts of Bnei Akiva.[36] My grandparents remained dislocated and ideologically indifferent, foreigners in a place they never recognized as their own. What united them all was the past: a past they were at once eager to forget and unable to let go of.

Upon their arrival in Palestine/Israel in 1949, my grandparents, together with my grandmother's sister and brother, were sent to Yahud, a newly constructed town in the central part of the country, built hurriedly over the ruins of the evacuated Palestinian village al-Abbasiyya. The irony never escaped them. They were refugees who were saved and given homes after years of suffering, hunger, and displacement, but those homes belonged to people who were now refugees.

Tsipe, the only one who ever talked about this explicitly, said she "didn't like the idea," but she was tired of running, "and besides, the war taught her that one's redemption is always another's downfall."

Tsipe and Hirschel never really left the war days even when they settled in Yahud. They remained refugees all their lives. They ate boiled potatoes and onions "because that is what they were used to," they hardly interacted with non–family members because "you cannot trust anyone," and they spoke only Yiddish because "Hebrew was for prayer, not for speaking."

No doubt my father grew up in a traumatized household. The transgenerational trauma passed quietly from parents to children without once being spoken about openly. He, and likely I too, inherited the fear of annihilation not just as a spoken legacy but at an epigenetic cellular level. Likely this was the source of our cathartic joy in sharing imaginary games like the "Gestapo Game."

Yahud was considered an underdeveloped periphery. Most of its new, Jewish inhabitants were Turkish, and just a few were Polish, especially those who were registered, like my family, as "other" because they came from Kazakhstan or Uzbekistan and had no Polish papers with them. German and other Jewish refugees from the main cities in Western Europe were settled in Tel Aviv, Jerusalem, or Haifa and soon became the emerging Israeli social, cultural, and political elite. My grandparents were not that kind of Polish Jew. They were poor and uneducated. They raised chickens and sold eggs for a living. Their world was, and remained throughout their lives in Israel, the world of the shtetl. A world of Yiddish jokes, daily prayer, proverbs, and hardship.

Fear and suspicion were instilled deeply in their minds and bodies over the years of escaping, hiding, being captive, and forced to work in inhumane conditions. They continued to live like fugitives, even when they could finally stop running. They managed to escape Poland in time to avoid the concentration camps, so they weren't "typical" Holocaust survivors. But they certainly lived in the shadow of that historical trauma. This must have contributed to my father's own clinical paranoia. How could it have not?

The Hochbergs remained foreign implants in their new home. They accepted their new lives in Yahud, as one accepts a necessity, but they didn't seem to have either adapted or made any effort to belong. "It was an arrangement" that they accepted as a lesser evil; they worked hard and survived. They had no further aspirations. I could see, even as a very young kid, that they had no plans, no hope, no joy. They focused on one thing only: surviving. This was the darkness my father grew up into, and while he did quite well for a while, their trauma, running through his veins, caught up with him over time.

Still, as a child, he was known as "The King of Yahud!" I grew up listening to the cousins and to his stories about these early days. He would talk about his childhood with bravado. I enjoyed seeing him puff up with pride recalling his adventures. He told me about his academic success but also about his street fights, his escapes from home, his bruises, and all the trouble he caused. He was as proud of the latter as he was of the former. "All the kids in Yahud feared and respected me," he would say. "I fooled them all! . . . I'd beat them up!"

Tsipe and Hirschel, like Bluma and Duvid, tried their best to make a home in Israel. They slowly picked up enough Hebrew to be able to sell eggs and get by. At some point, Tsipe moved on and opened a small kiosk where she sold candy to all of Yahud's children: "No cigarettes, just candy and peanuts." The small, simple world of Yahud, a marginal, poor suburb back then, was my father's kingdom.

I was excited about the forthcoming meeting with his cousins. I hadn't seen them in a decade, and they were my ticket into a past I otherwise had no access to. *How ironic*, I thought to myself, *that I, a total outsider, am the one to get them together, the cousins who all live in Israel, not too far from each other, and still somehow never meet. Unless there is a funeral or a wedding.* But, in a way, it also felt natural. I was, after all, *his* daughter, and *he* was their leader. The leader of the tribe. I felt it was my duty to gather them, given that my father—their childhood hero—was the first to die, and this after losing his mind, his job, his respect, and his legacy.

They must have felt let down, even betrayed by him: Their mighty hero, "King of Yahud," "the famous worldly professor," falling out of glory, leaving them with nothing to be proud of. From being the firstborn, the leader of the tribe, the gifted boy, and the pride of the family, he became the sickly madman they struggled to understand and had no idea how to mourn. I knew they felt shame. I knew it, because I did too.

The meeting was set. We would meet at Batia's in Petach Tikvah for dinner. The cousins told me they would all bring photos. Haim picked me up, and we drove over together. As we got closer, I began to feel my heart racing. My father would have been seventy-seven now. I imagined him joining us at the dinner table at Batia's apartment.

As I entered the house, right into a warm hug from Batia, I was surprised by just how natural and familiar it all felt. As if ten years hadn't passed. As if I didn't live on the other side of the world. As if our daily and mental realities (theirs one of observant Jews, Zionists, with tens of grandchildren and even great-grandchildren) and mine (a queer, secular woman, an openly anti-Zionist Jew living in the United States for two decades) didn't exist. Or, if they did, they absolutely did not matter. We were family and the ease was enticing.

Batia, seventy-four, her sister Leah, seventy-two, Haim, seventy-five, Benny, seventy-one, and Yossi, his brother, seventy, were all there. They looked absolutely the same to me as they did when I was a kid and they were in their late twenties and thirties. They looked old to me back then, but now, the twenty-year age gap between us hardly mattered. Funny how age appears different through a child's eyes: Once "old" in my eyes, they now seemed firmly ageless. As if time had stood still, I felt I was again the little girl, Gilly, surrounded by her father's loving cousins. It was comforting.

The cousins brought photos from their shared childhood in Yahud, and we all sat at the coffee table and passed them around. My father's absence filled the room and made him the natural center of conversation. The cousins shared stories and memories, while I wrote everything down:

"No one else was like him. He was funny, smart, and wild. Once he broke into the synagogue and..."

"All the girls were in love with him. I still meet women who remember him. He was so charismatic."

"No one knew what was bigger, his brain or his ego," Haim commented. The cousins smiled nervously. They got the snarky comment, and they didn't like it. I listened, drinking in all this information, trying to absorb as much of their love and admiration of him into myself so I could imagine him there, in the room with us. This man, who was my childhood hero, was also theirs. With them, I could feel the magnitude of my loss. He was a giant—and giants are not supposed to become so small, so sick, so lost.

We moved to the dining table for dinner. Haim brought trays of sushi from his favorite Japanese restaurant in Tel Aviv. Leah, Batia, and their husbands had never had sushi before. "Menachem, is this kosher?" Leah asked. They called their son, the rabbi, to consult. "We can have the cooked salmon one and the tuna. Don't eat the rest."

Batia served homemade chicken soup, a potato knish, and salad. The clash between the sushi and the rest of the food made me smile. Where else would

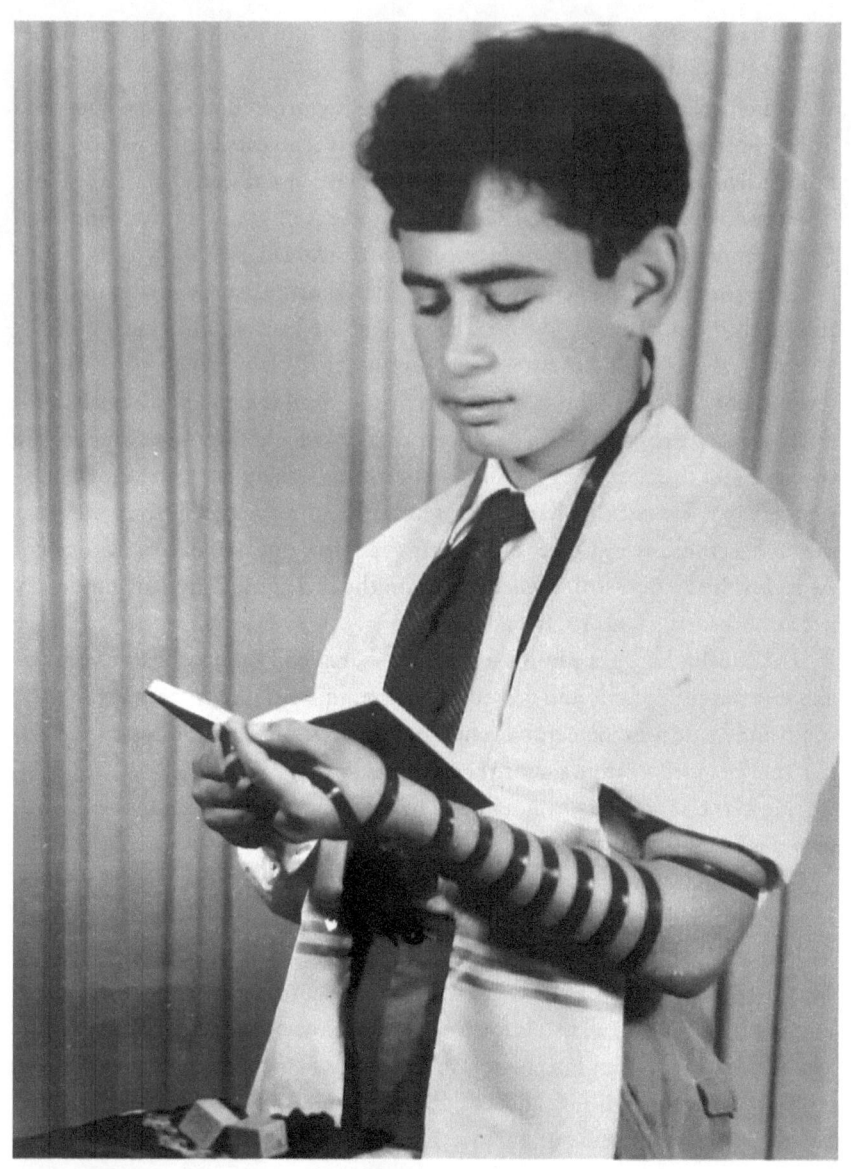
"King of Yahud": my dad's bar mitzvah. Yahud, 1958.

you find this food combination served for dinner? After a short while, Batia pushed away the sushi ("I can't eat this, it is uncooked!"). Haim told them they needed to catch up with the spirit of the times. They smiled. "Things you do in Tel Aviv are not how we live here," Batia answered, "but it looks like Menachem is enjoying this," she added. "I never liked the smell of seaweed. Not for me." She pushed the tray away.

I took another piece of the knish. "Tastebuds are developed in childhood. I never got used to eating raw fish."

"Your loss, y'all!" Haim concluded and gulped down another piece of sushi. We all laughed.

"Tell me more about your parents," I asked. "I know so little about our family history."

Batia jumped right in, as if she was waiting for this question all along. She leaned back in her seat and took on the role of narrator: "So you know, they were five kids. They lived with their parents in Krasnobród, which was a small Jewish town near Lublin. They were very poor and their father died young, which is why Dov, the oldest brother, left for Łódź to work and send money back. No one knows what happened to him. In 1939, when the Nazis came, the younger siblings asked him to run away with them, but he refused. They never found him again. Your grandmother was now the eldest, so she, their mother, my mother Bluma, and their younger brothers, Sholem and Duvid, managed to cross the border from east Poland to Russia. They were asked to give up their Polish citizenship and take a Russian one, but they refused. So they were sent to Siberia as Polish prisoners of war to cut wood and build railroads. They had little to eat, they were cold and hungry, but happy to survive. Many others perished. In 1941, they and all other Polish citizens were released from Siberia. They thought the 'hell is over.' They had no idea it was just the beginning."

"I am amazed I knew none of this," I interrupted. "I must say, abba never told me a thing about any of this."

"Our parents didn't talk about it," Leah responded. "They didn't want us to grow up with their memories. They wanted to forget. For them, life began in 1949 and nothing before that was worth remembering."

"Our mother was different," Haim jumped in. "She used to tell us that *our* life began in 1949 but *hers* ended in 1939."

"Cheerful message," I responded and smiled.

"Tsipe was never a cheerful woman," Yossi added.

"My mother," Haim muttered, "didn't want to live. I don't blame her, their life was so difficult, but Bluma was always more optimistic."

Tsipe was dark, and her sister Bluma seemed so cheerful. I remember this vividly. As a child visiting my grandparents, I always hoped Bluma would visit. She lived nearby, and when she did come, my grandparents' depressing apartment would be filled with life and light.

One story my dad loved telling was that "she gave birth to him all alone, sitting on a toilet seat in a labor camp in Kazakhstan." The story, and how he told it, emphasized her loneliness and strength as much as it did the fact that he was born into a toilet. Both aspects were equally important. When I suggested the story didn't make sense, he replied: "That is because you don't know how proud and strong your *savta* was. She *chose* the toilet, because it was the only place she could find privacy."

I did know she was proud. Proud, bitter, and unhappy. She was also unhealthy.

She had three open heart surgeries before her heart gave up and she died. I remember visiting her in the hospital just before leaving for Berkeley to begin my PhD program. He was there, too. We came to share the news. He told her, "Gilly is going to California, on her way to get a PhD in literature." She opened her gray, watery eyes, stared right at us both as if we were the bearers of terrible news, and said: "Doctor *le-spharim* [a doctor of books]. That is no better than doctor *le-misparim* [doctor of numbers]." She wasn't trying to be funny by using the Hebrew rhyming words. She was dead serious and dismissive. She was nearing her death, in pain, in the hospital, and she expressed her frustration with both of us. She made it clear: "Bravo. Doctors of *Misparim* [numbers] and *Sipurim* [stories]. How is that going to help anyone? Not a single real doctor: doctor *shel anashim* [a doctor of people]!" The two of us stood by her bed. We came with what we thought was good news that would make her proud. But she made it clear that we'd both failed her.

Tsipe wasn't an easy woman to be around, and I wasn't close to her. Even so, as I was growing up, she made a point of teaching me a few lessons. These left a great and lasting impact on me. The first lesson, which she repeated over the years, was that "all rich people are thieves." She explained this by saying that "the only way some people become very rich is that they don't mind stealing from others." The second lesson, delivered in a similar feisty spirit, was that "Jesus was the only real socialist and all the rest were fake." She mentioned this often, explaining the "Israeli labor movement was *fakakta*." I grew up with these lessons, which strongly shaped my skeptical outlook and my distaste for capitalism.

So, yes, I surely knew Tsipe was proud. She was also strong and uncompromising and had a very clear and harshly binary assessment of the world: There

Family photos and medical documents. Displaced persons camp, Germany, collected 1947–49.

were good things and good people and bad things and bad people. There were Jews and there were Poles. There were rich and unethical and there were poor and virtuous. There were smart and there were stupid. Then there was our grandfather, Hirschel. He, she deemed, was "a good, poor Jew but stupid." Still, she made sure we knew that "stupid was better than bad and greedy," even if it wasn't good enough.

"Enough with that!" I was awakened from my short rumination by Batia's voice, which cut through forcefully. "Let me continue the story." She raised her voice, pulling our attention back to her.

"After they were released from prison in Siberia, they made their way east to Uzbekistan. They'd lost the little security they had: bread and shelter. They had no work permits, without which they had no means to eat. We don't know how they survived, but they managed to get to Kazakhstan, where conditions were better. Finally, they had work, food, and warmer clothes. Your grandmother married Hirschel and your father was born. They always said that Kazakhstan was 'their time of glory.' Then the war ended. 1945. They thought they were going back home..."

"Back home?!" Leah interrupted again. "What home! Lo bait ve-lo na'alim [no home, no shoes]. Imakh shmam shel ha-polanim [Damn those Poles]!" All five cousins nodded their heads in agreement. I grew up hearing that "Poles are the worst. Worse than Germans."

Batia quieted everyone and continued. She seemed determined to deliver the details as accurately as possible. "Finally, someone is going to write this all down," she said. "Yosef's daughter! Of course. Another professor. Smart, just like her father. Kol hakavod [Write it down]!" She pointed at the paper before me and continued: "In 1945, they went back to their town in Poland to find it destroyed. All their Jewish neighbors were dead. They managed to escape to Czechoslovakia, and from there to Austria, and finally to Germany, where they settled in a displaced persons camp. They lived there from 1946 to 1949. That is where I was born. Where Leah was born. Haim and Benny, too. We were all born in refugee camps. Then, in 1949, they made it to Israel on a boat. There. Now you know everything. Now you know how we got here."

"Have you ever gone back to visit?" I asked. "Poland? Germany?"

"Chas ve-chalila [heaven forbid]," Batia answered. "What do I have to look for there? There is nothing for us there but *mavet* [death]. We are here now. This is our life. This is our home."

"Barukh-hashem, Barukh-hashem," all five cousins mumbled. Then Batia poured a little kosher red wine in our glasses. We lifted our wine glasses, and Batia said: "To Yossi's memory!"

"Le-chaim! Le-chaim," we all said as we clinked our glasses and sipped. "Le-chaim," I heard myself say as I drifted into a childhood memory.

Le-Yossi!

"Lama le-chaim?" my dad asked as the two of us sat down for dinner and lifted our Coca-Cola-filled wine glasses to toast. We were enjoying one of his magical homemade dinners in his trailer in Bloomington, Indiana. The times when he transformed "nothing into something." We were having grilled cheese sandwiches with a special twist: He added corn from a can and green peas to the mix—"It's good to have vegetables!"

As we lifted our glasses to toast, I said, "Le-chaim!"

"Why to Chaim and not to Yossi?" he asked, smiling. *Le-chaim* means "to life," but Chaim/Haim is also his younger brother's name. We both got the joke. "From now on, you and I say 'le-Yossi,'" he added and put on a victorious expression.

"Hahaha," we laughed, and I lifted my glass high up in the air and yelled, "Le-Yossi!" and then, "Le-abba Yossi!"

This eleven-year-old laughing kid, sitting with her dad and toasting him, had no idea that he, while joking, was also, most likely, also a bit serious. She had no idea that for him, *Le-chaim* had always been a sign of some cosmic injustice. He wrote about it in a note I found and read forty years later, after his death:

Why was I named Yosef [He who adds] if I was the firstborn? And why was he named Chaim [life], as if he was the source of vitality?

He asked this in writing but never answered. He left the question open, as he did many other questions. Questions that bothered him, made him feel paranoid, dishonored, unseen, disrespected. His frustration mounted and became more visible the more I read his texts: He was angry with his partners who failed him and with the cosmos that allowed this to happen.

The eleven-year-old didn't know that her dad was seriously preoccupied with the matter of the Jewish toast, just like he was with all matters pertaining to his place and status in the world. For her, "le-Yossi" was just a joke they shared back then. For him, it was a corrective act of great magnitude. One of many.

She didn't know (how could she?) that her funny, lovable dad lived his entire life torn apart by an innate sense of injustice and relentless competition: Why his brother and not him? Why anyone and not him? He first tried to overcome his inferiority complex and feed his megalomaniac drive by becoming "the best statistician in the world," as he'd told his future wife on first meeting her. His ambition proved fruitful. He became a very successful biostatistician, indeed, among the leading figures in the field. But it wasn't enough. Nothing was enough. Nothing could provide the affirmation he was seeking, night and day, that he was "the one," "the best," "the only." Without that constant affirmation, he sank, fast. Sliding rapidly and repeatedly from the heights of euphoria to the rock bottom of despair.

Is this why he had to become the Messiah? Joining the messianic fervor that swept the entire nation? Was that his answer to his ongoing sense of failure?

Failure to achieve certain things and, even more so, the failures of others to recognize the full magnitude of his achievements.

May 2023 | 1949–1963
New York · Israeli Army Prison, Yahud

A Jewish Jean Genet

Back in New York City, after the moving meeting with the cousins and filled with tender childhood memories, I was determined to find out more about my father's formative years. His childhood and his youth. I perused some of the earliest writings in my possession. 1963. In the narrow, faded, off-white page he had scribbled a few notes about meeting an Italian girl on a boat trip he took as part of an international youth delegation to the United Nations: "She was my ticket to the *real* world."

I'd heard the story about him being chosen to represent Israel in the first Israeli youth delegation to the United Nations many times. He was very proud of it. But now, as I read his own description, I realized for the first time how transformative this journey overseas had been for him.

> Today I took off my kippah and threw it in the ocean. I am free! I am done with all the superstitions my parents believe in. That belongs to Yahud. The world is bigger and I am bigger. When we get to shore, I will eat pork and then we will see if the sky opens and I die, as my mother always warned me. Primitive thoughts.

I smiled as I read the last line. I too had grown up fearing the idea of eating pork. My fear has always been profound enough that even though I am not, by any means, an observant Jew, I never ate it. Nor have I allowed my kids to eat it. "Better not take a chance. You never know. Jehovah is known to have a bad temperament. He can get really nasty when he's crossed."

I picked up another one of his early notes. This one simply stated: "When I get back, I'm going to leave the yeshiva for good. My poor mom. I'm going to be drafted to the army."

"The world is bigger, and I am bigger": My dad as a participant in an international youth delegation to the United Nations. New York, 1963.

The army?! I mean, yes, everyone in Israel must serve, but somehow, I never thought about my father in the army.[37] He never mentioned it, and it never occurred to me to ask. I simply couldn't imagine him as a soldier. I decided to send Haim a WhatsApp message: "Hi, Haim. Hope you are well. Listen, I'm reading some of abba's writings and he mentions the army. Did he actually serve? I realize I never heard about those years from him."

Within minutes, Haim wrote back: "Hi, Gilly. Let's put it this way. Whatever he did or didn't do in the army, it wasn't for long. He was drafted but very soon after released. I think he served five months of the three-year compulsory service, and most of that time in an army jail."

Our texting continued for a while longer: "He was in jail?!"

"Yes. But he hid it from our parents. And we never talked about it."

"Why was he in jail?"

"Disobedience. Something about beating up an officer. I don't actually know the details. Yossi never wanted to talk about it."

I was unable to find out anything more. Haim shared the little he knew. I called my mom and asked her about it. She too said she knew nothing about what actually happened during his short army service, but she mentioned that when the two of them met as young students at Tel Aviv University, my dad proudly told her that he "tricked his way into the university." She said, "He told me that he was able to get into the university because he managed to get into the IDF archive, steal his file, get rid of any evidence of his misbehavior and jail time, replacing it with fake documents that facilitated his admission." She added that she was "very impressed with him back then" but had no idea if any of these stories were true: "No one knew with your dad. He loved telling bravado stories about himself. He did this, he did that. He fooled, he tricked, he managed to bypass all limitations because he was always smarter than anyone else. Over time, spending years with him, I learned most of his stories were total fabrications. So, I have no idea if he ever served and, if he did, what he did or didn't do in the army."

No one seemed to know, and my dad's writings provided no answer to these questions. I did, however, find a few poems he had written during that period. They were written on torn pieces of military-issued paper, marked: "Kele 6"—IDF Army Jail 6. I had no idea he wrote poetry as an eighteen-year-old, but now I had clear evidence confirming that he had indeed spent time in an Israeli army jail.

How wild, I thought to myself. Not every day does one find poems written on jail stationery. He was just over eighteen at the time, writing in his prison cell. *How did he find the motivation to write poetry in prison?* I asked myself as I translated his naively youthful Hebrew into English. I couldn't help but think he dated them and titled them as "prison poems" because he wanted them to be found and reveal his tormented, poetic soul.

> I watch the fading fire
> and see the water splash
> And there is no war.
> I watch the long waves
> and see his long arms
> Hugging his back
> And there is no war
> But his back is too small for peace
> So, he waves his arms for war
> until tired, they fall down
> Like long shadows
> Dead
> "Kele 6" (Prison 6), 24/1/1963

> Today I hide
> not a single sun ray will enter
> Soon night will fall
> my eyes are already tired
> No light
> maybe in the dark
> I will break through the doors
> "Kele 6" (Prison 6), 1963

I found eight more poems. They all conceal more than they reveal. But as I translated, reread, and traced his handwritten words, I began to feel his presence strongly. I sensed his youthful breath through the curve of the letters, the diagonal leftward slant of his writing. He is still here, in the ink. In the materiality left by his shaky handwriting. I close my eyes and try to imagine him: young, skinny, sitting on the narrow, metal cell bed, covered by a stiff wool military blanket. I imagine his legs are curled up toward his chest and he is holding the pen in his right hand, the paper in his left. He is about to write a poem. I imagine he saw himself as a romantic back then: He was an imprisoned poet. A rebel without a cause. A misfit. A tortured soul. A Jewish Jean Genet.

Yeshiva Boy by Day, Gangster by Night

I decided to go further back to revisit and reread many of his texts to learn more about his childhood. I'd already read them all during the pandemic years, but for the most part they left me without a clear picture of his youth. Written as riddles filled with ambiguities and uncertainties, these texts, time and again, confirmed only that from his early childhood through to high school in the yeshiva and into his university studies, he was always told by his entire family that he was "number one." "He was the king," and his mother especially instilled in him a sense of "being chosen."

"Your dad was a wild boy," my grandmother once told me. The two of us were sitting in her small kitchen drinking warm milk and eating her homemade sugar cookies. I loved watching her dip the hard cookie in the milk and then suck on it. She used to boil eggs in the milk, explaining, "If I am already boiling the milk, it is better to use it for making eggs. Why waste water on that?" She talked about my dad all the time. "He was always so smart, Yosale." I don't remember her ever talking about anything else. Her favorite topic of conversation, however, wasn't my dad's brightness but how much he made her worry. She could go on for hours: "He would leave the house at dawn, in his school uniform and kippah, looking all respectable and mature like a good yeshiva bocher. Then as soon as he got back home, he would take off the nice clothes, throw off the kippah, and run outside looking for trouble. He kept me up, night after night. I was always dead worried. Then he would come back, covered with mud and blood. He always got into fights, my Yosale."

Haim too had always liked sharing stories about my dad's youth. "Your dad was a wild boy, a criminal really," he told me on more than one occasion. "Everyone in Yahud respected and feared him. Adults and kids. He was king of Yahud! He was everything: a yeshiva boy by day, a gangster by night!"

I grew up with this legacy. *Yeshiva boy by day, gangster by night.* I knew that at twelve he won a scholarship to the prestigious yeshiva school T'saitlin in Tel Aviv, while his childhood friends, cousins, and his brother Haim stayed in the underfunded public school in Yahud. Most of them never finished high school. He would leave the neighborhood early every morning, dressed in his school uniform, and take the bus to the big city, returning in the early evening. He was "the gifted one" and gained authority over the rest of the kids, and even adults. He made it. They all treated him with respect but also with fear. He was just as famous for being smart as he was for being hot-tempered, impulsive, and violent.

That is how I came to understand him over time. He was a man of extremes and a tormented soul. He had a light side and a dark side. We all do. But his extremes frequently reached extremes. I had a sense of this yeshiva/gangster duality from early on, but I didn't really know how to relate to it or match it with the image of the "fun, summer vacation dad" I had growing up. I knew and didn't know; I sensed and didn't sense his explosive side.

My dad must have grown up with fantasies of grandeur: He was the greatest, the best, the smartest, the strongest, the "king of Yahud!" The only one of the family who had a chance of "making it in the real world." And if he couldn't be that, he had to become nothing at all. I called my mother to ask her about this, and she eagerly confirmed: "Your dad was convinced he was the closest thing to God on this planet. He had to be number one. Always, everywhere, at everything. And if he wasn't, he would go crazy, throw things at the wall. He was scary!"

I have no recollection of any such events. But I know that, as a child, I certainly had a sense that at any given moment my father could move from a good mood to sudden tears or anger. It was my job to "keep him calm." So, when he told me that the planetarium right next to campus was his "private tennis ball," or that he could "shrink things and make them grow huge again," or that he could "see through walls," I never challenged him.

I never knew if he was serious or playing, but I sensed it would be wiser not to inquire. I just pretended to believe all those grandiose things he told me about himself. I loved his fantastic sense of his own superpowers, but, more importantly, I wanted to keep him happy. I knew, without knowing, that "this would be better for us all."

As an adult, I came to see he wasn't just a self-loving megalomaniac who believed he had superpowers. Quite the opposite: He was in torment, pulled and pushed by an acute sense of empowerment on the one hand and self-loathing on the other. Without his fantasy of godlike superiority, he folded into total abjection. And so he kept falling from the heights of his inflated ego to the abysmal depths of depressive hell, time and time again. He managed to hide his internal war for a long time while under the professorial persona he constructed. Until he no longer could.

2023–2024

New York

Messianic Jargon, or Lessons of a Madman

I had now read all his short stories and poems. I had to sadly conclude that my father was not a hidden literary prodigy. The stories aren't terrible, but they're far from good. And the poems? Having a mother as a published poet raises the bar. Reading his poetry in comparison to hers does injustice to his youthful musings, but I cannot help it. I decided to end my engagement with his literary endeavors. I moved on to the few remaining texts I had not yet read. Most of these, especially the ones he wrote from the late 1990s on, unfolded his inner world made of secret omens, miracles, vows, and echoes of past words and citations: biblical, rabbinic, Hebrew, Aramaic.

I am startled by the force of my father's belief in the superiority of what he called "Jewish life" and his adamant rejection of anything he considered "Christian influence": science, Western philosophy, analytical thinking, statistics (!). This surely comes across as the unifying trend across all his writings since 1991, the year he began to live in and out of the psychiatric ward. If he was indeed mad, he was very systematic in his madness.

During the decade beginning in 1991 and ending in 2002, he was teaching on and off. He was on medical leave during his depressive states and periods of hospitalization, and then he was back in the classroom. His tenure secured his position, and while his colleagues and students at the university had surely sensed something was wrong, they went along with it, pretending that everything was business as usual. It wasn't. For the longest time, no one said anything. Finally, in 2002, one brave PhD student complained: "He doesn't teach us statistics, he just rambles about his mathematical proof of God's existence, about *hitgalut* [revelation], and about the Messiah." The student filed an official complaint, which led to an investigation and eventually forced "early retirement." From then on, my father never set foot on campus again. He was fifty-eight when his career as a professor ended.

For the remaining eleven years of his life, he kept to a regular cycle: waves of deep depression followed by intensive psychiatric treatment leading to improvement. Then, once he felt good enough, he would stop his treatment, which led to manic outbursts and a new period of messianic delusions. During these periods, I would discover as his postmortem reader, he would write feverishly to

God, about God. Most of his writings from the last two decades of his life are filled with messianic jargon. Reading them is like entering a mind on fire. Still, his thoughts are systematized and coherent, following a clear logic, even if it is an outlandishly uncompromised, binary one: There is "a Jewish way of living and a Christian way of living," "Jewish belief OR science," "Jewish people and goyim," "real Messiah or fake ones (Jesus)."

He is committed to "an authentic Jewish life," which is also why he must stop being a scientist and leave the university, why he must never read Western philosophy, why the only books he should keep on his shelves are Jewish *kitvie kodesh*, and why he must not listen to doctors or take pills but instead trust God, "for he alone is one's healer and curer." Many of his texts are written as lists or pamphlets. The tone is instructive and dogmatic.

February 2003.

Facts and some actions required by the People of Israel to assure the arrival of the Messiah and the victory of the Jewish authentic way of life:

1. Every Jew has the potential to become the Messiah and must be ready to take on the position if chosen.
2. All Jews must come forward and nominate themselves for this position of servitude.
3. All Jews must liberate themselves from the Christian mind by no longer reading Western philosophy.
4. All Jews must know why Moses and Aaron failed God and learn from their failure:

"Moses and Aaron did not sanctify the name of God because they failed to say, as God ordered them: *This rock will bring forth water for you.*"

5. A true Messiah must not fail. A true Messiah must do as God orders.
6. I, Yosef Hochberg, am not going to fail. I nominated myself to the position of true Messiah and here is my vow:

This professor of statistics will bring forth the Messiah for you.

7. I also vow to do my very best to help my daughter. She lives among the goyim and studies philosophy. She reads Kant and Hegel. I am afraid she is already a Christian. I shall do my very best to bring her back to *darchey ha-shem* [the Path of God].

I was surprised and moved, if saddened by the dismissal of my academic journey, to find myself referenced here. By 2003, my father and I were hardly in touch. I moved from Berkeley to Los Angeles to begin my first academic work at UCLA, joining the Department of Comparative Literature as a fresh assistant professor. When I told him about it, he said, "When will you wake up and see there is only one thing you must do: Follow God's ways and settle in the Promised Land." Back then I thought (or wanted to believe) he was joking. He wasn't.

For him, "I was almost lost." In my mind, it was clearly *he* who was already lost. Lost to madness I couldn't fathom. Madness that terrified me. I suppose we lost each other. He considered my academic career to be a form of conversion and betrayal. I became a professor in 2002, the same year he was forced into retirement. The year he declared all academic work, science, and Western philosophy to be sinful and to be in contrast to authentic Jewish life. "In God alone you must trust!" I find time and again in his writings from the period, as he rejects all lessons of the Enlightenment and the "arrogance of men believing in the supremacy of the human mind."

As I read his words, I remember clearly how, back when he dismissed my new academic career, I found comfort in reminding myself he "was crazy" and told myself to ignore him. Now as I read him, with my own increasing skepticism about the capacities and importance of analytic thinking (not because of theological belief but because of my growing attraction to creative nonanalytical ways of thinking), I find his rejection of Western philosophy and the reasoning mind significantly more interesting. I can even relate to his passionate attachment to messianic impulses and modes of expression. I am reminded of the much-celebrated lines from Walter Benjamin's "Theses on the Philosophy of History": "We know that the Jews were prohibited from investigating the future. The Torah and the prayers instruct them in remembrance, however. This stripped the future of its magic, to which all those succumb who turn to the soothsayers for enlightenment. This does not imply, however, that for the Jews the future turned into homogeneous, empty time. For every second of time was the strait gate through which Messiah might enter."[38]

I wonder, as I reread these words, if, as readers of Benjamin, we have read them in their own right or if we have subjected them to a Christian (Cartesian and Enlightened) philosophical framework and understanding of temporality. How would my dad have read them? I try to find comfort in this thought, because it suggests that maybe he wasn't altogether "just crazy." Maybe, like Benjamin, he had a point.

My Queerness, Divine Intervention

I knew my queerness never threatened my dad. Not when I was a child and couldn't yet express it, not when I was an adult and came out to him. My sexuality didn't seem to preoccupy him at all (unlike my graduate studies and my interest in Kant and Hegel, which he found alarming). But I didn't know what he thought about it, or whether he thought about it at all, later in life, when he became mentally ill, when he reembraced Judaism in its most national, fundamental incarnation, or when he nominated himself to the position of the Messiah, eventually convinced he was chosen. It therefore warmed my heart to find among his texts a note from 2000 in which he explicitly addressed my queerness and even considered it "a blessing"—indeed, "God's direct response to his plea." My queerness, I learned, is no less than a sign of God's good will. It is no less than a mark of divine intervention. My father wrote:

August 8, 2000

Thank you, *Hashem, boreh olam* [Thank you God, world creator]

I am writing to you now, at 4:33 a.m., because I cannot sleep. Today I had a long phone conversation with my daughter Gilly, who now lives in Berkeley among the goyim. I raised her to know the ways of the Jews and the prayers and the blessings. She knows them all by heart, I am certain of that. But she does not follow any mitzvot. She doesn't even light the Shabbat candles. I have tried to correct her ways, but alas, I cannot. So, Elohim, I ask that despite her behavior, you shall continue to protect her, for I am truly worried about her. You have been kind to her in the past, and I hope you will help her again. I already thanked you for making her a lesbian, to save her from suffering. I immediately understood this was your great plan. For you did not want her to continue to be unhappy with men as she was. You knew her misery and you made her gay. Only you, the one and only, knows the ways of human hearts. And only you, the one and only, could have come up with such a brilliant solution to her sorrow. I am thankful to you for her personal redemption. I pray for you to lead her back to her people and back to you, for in you alone I trust.

My father, a religious man, a mentally ill man, a delusional, manic, self-appointed Messiah, might have been crazy, but he loved me. And unlike my bohemian-secular-poet mother, who refused to accept my queerness until at least a decade after I first came out to her, he found a way to turn my gayness into a sign of God's greatness. He came up with a theological explanation for my sexual orientation and even thanked God for it. Most importantly, he wanted me to be happy. As he saw it, my queerness was my redemption. How beautiful is that?

Miracles

It was a Sunday, end of May, late afternoon. I was in my study again, reading him, when I ground to a halt. I found my name again, this time in one of his earlier writings about the forthcoming redemption. Every time I saw my name in his later texts, I was surprised he assigned me a place in his well-crafted messianic cosmos. I was moved to tears to see how much he cared about me but saddened to discover how much my disbelief in his visions and my dismissal of his worldview had hurt him.

18/11/1996

Kislev, the Hebrew month of miracles.

My daughter, Gilly, doesn't believe in the coming redemption. It is sad to me because she must know that *geula* [redemption] is not just an abstract concept and that it includes personal redemption. I don't understand why, despite the fact that she knows well that my belief in *geula* is firm, she remains skeptical. I think it is because she is reading too many Christian philosophers in California where she is getting her PhD. She should instead be reading *ketvie kodesh* [sacred Jewish texts]. I talked to her and reassured her that I personally promise her *own redemption* by the age of thirty. Still, she refuses to believe! However, as her loving father, I decided to ignore her chutzpah. I continue to do everything in my capacity to fulfill my promise to her. She may not believe in miracles, but I do. Just yesterday I noticed a miracle (and immediately knew I must tell her!). A plastic bottle of water, which was sitting for hours in the heated car, turned ice-cold the minute I touched it. I wrote an email to her, telling her about this miracle with great excitement. She responded by making fun of me. She rhymed and made a perfect Hebrew biblical statement: *"abba hoze, abba chose"* [dad the delirious, dad the oracle]. She is witty but she never takes me seriously. I forgive her because I love her. For now, I will have to ignore her skepticism and continue on my path. I know her personal redemption is coming, whether she believes it or not.

My father was right, I never believed in miracles and never thought he could predict my future. I never believed in redemption, not mine or anyone else's.

Still, he and I shared a special bond, and Judaism, at least *his* version of it, surely was part of it. His world of miracles, divine interventions, Hasidic songs, biblical figures, and stories of might and redemption were a key part of my upbringing, my childhood, and they came to serve as an outlet for my playful queerness long before I knew I was gay. It is only now, after these long years of reading him and writing about and with him, that I came to really see how central this "Jewish" part of my upbringing has always been to me, personally and for our special bond.

Now, as I walk through my current world in New York City, this fantastic cosmopolitan city, through my queer lifestyle, as a professor at an Ivy League university, a citizen of the world, a typical intellectual, I feel, perhaps for the first time ever, at a cellular level, that I am perhaps not the secular person I've always thought myself to be. *But what does this mean?* What does it mean for me, now, a queer woman, a New Yorker, a professor, a person who doesn't observe anything, who hates the high holidays and avoids the synagogue at all costs, what does religion mean to me? And what, more specifically, does "being Jewish" mean to me?

My Jewishness has very little to do with organized religion and even less to do with national expression. It is a very personal experience. But I refuse to call it "cultural," a term American Jews invented. I'm not even sure I know what it means. My Jewishness is not cultural because I don't know what of my cultural experience is in fact Jewish. My Jewishness is very private and intimate. I do not experience it as a public affair or in the context of a cultural setting. My Jewishness, I've come to see, is above all about my special bond with my father. My Jewishness has always been a way to connect to him, a means to create and express with him. My Jewishness is part of the taste of my childhood. It is early memories of him and me together. It informs the sweetest of all my childhood memories: dancing with him, singing with him, playing with him. As such, it is not cultural. It is fundamental to who I am at my very core: my bodily expressions, my voice, my nostalgia, expressivity, humor, primary emotional attachments.

When my two kids were born, three years apart, in Los Angeles, far away from everything I grew up with—Israel, Judaism, Hebrew—I felt the need to share some of my childhood experiences with them. *But how?* Everything I tried felt wrong, inauthentic, misplaced. When they were very young, I sent them to a Reform Jewish Sunday school in Los Angeles and even joined the congregation. I hated the ceremonies that felt fake (and I never understood why everyone was wearing white clothes all the time, as if that marked some state of holiness or purity or respect for the almighty). Eli and Omri on their part hated Hebrew school and rebelled forcefully. At first, I insisted. "It's important that they have a sense of Jewish identity," I said, when my partner Keri suggested that we stop forcing them to go. Eventually I accepted their pleas. After all, this kind of American Reform Judaism was totally foreign to me and had absolutely nothing to do with the Hasidic songs I shared with my dad or the games we played. There was no point in trying to force this form of Judaism on them. It didn't even feel Jewish to me.

A few years later, I discovered a small community of anti-Zionist, socialist Jews who congregated every Shabbat not far from us in West Los Angeles. They sang in Yiddish and read the history of the Jewish Bund.[39] This was totally foreign to me, but I considered their strong support of unions and anti-Zionist politics to be an asset. I figured if the kids joined their Bund Kids Club of LA, they would at least learn important lessons about social justice from a secular Jewish point of view. Eli and Omri went three times. They learned a couple of Yiddish socialist songs, after which their resistance mounted again: "We don't want to go there!" I gave up and let it go. After all, it wasn't "tradition" or "identity" I wanted to pass on to them. It was the experience of my childhood with my dad, and that was an experience no organized setting, whether reformed Judaism or Jewish socialism, could possibly replicate. It was an irreplaceable miracle.

Growing up in Israel meant that Judaism was the norm, not a choice. It simply marked the order of public life: when vacations took place, what holidays were celebrated, what ethnonational stories were passed on as History with a capital H, what kinds of meat were available in standard markets and what kind of meat was found (secretively) only in very rare boutique delicatessens. My world, as I was growing up, was Jewish in the sense that my calendar was Jewish, everyone around me was Jewish, my school curriculum was Jewish, and I knew nothing else. But for my kids, growing up in the States, "being Jewish" felt like a fabricated story. They accepted it as their identity as long as this didn't tie them to anything beyond a few holiday celebrations. I too didn't really care for any official Jewish affiliations or ceremonies. What mattered to me was the very specific and personal experience I shared with my dad and that, I came to realize, was hardly something I could pass on to them. Certainly not through the public means available to me: reformed American Judaism, liberal Zionism, or, as I found out with time, more commonly the mixture of both.

We ended up doing away with the Hebrew school, high-holiday services, even bar mitzvahs and circumcision. None of these meant anything to me or to them. But I still wanted my dad's own joyful rendition of Judaism to be part of their lives, if indirectly. After all, it meant so much to him and to me. I wanted them to remember him, but he died when they were young. Too young to remember much. *How could I possibly make them remember a man they hardly knew? Or feel affinity to my childhood experience of Hasidic dancing and singing in Yiddish, something so remote and alienating for them?*

During the months we lived in Israel in 2012–2013, just before his sudden death, the kids and I visited him and Miriam almost weekly. Eli was seven, Omri was four, and neither of them liked going there because, as they said, "it smelled" and "it was boring!" By that time, my dad was already cognitively far gone, and he hardly engaged with us. We would arrive to find him seated in his armchair, his eyes devoid of expression, his dog, Lucky, sitting on his lap. The kids had no idea how to relate to this half-person-half-object "thing" called "*saba* Yossi" (grandpa). He/it made them nervous and they were restless to leave from the moment we'd arrived. Miriam dominated the scene, which followed the same routine each visit. We'd show up, Miriam would open the door and welcome us with a big fake smile. She'd offer cookies and give each kid a cheap gift (a drawing book, a plastic toy car). On rare occasions, if we got lucky, my dad would be a little more alert and attentive. Those were the good visits, when he noticed the kids' presence, even asked them a few questions about Los Angeles, about school, and what they wanted to do later in life. But more often than not, he didn't talk to us, and I wasn't sure if he noticed them at all.

Since he died, I've been telling Eli and Omri lots of stories about *saba* Yossi and all his wonders, hoping to keep his memory alive with them. I often regret that I didn't do enough to make sure they would get to know him better. Perhaps I should have tried harder. Perhaps we could have visited more often. *I should have made more effort to reconnect*, I tell myself. But then again, this is partially why I am writing this. It is my Jewish legacy.

Diet Poem

Foreign as my dad's messianic (inner) world was to me, his humor shines through, making this phantasmatic Jewish theological cosmology at times even entertaining. I could totally imagine the pleasure he found in writing some of his funnier texts. He used his mastery of biblical sources and his yeshiva upbringing to advance his personal war against science and what he called "Christian enlightenment." I read his polemics and thought, *He surely is not the only one to equate secularism, science, and analytic thinking with Christianity.* He did much of this with a sense of humor that I recognized as distinctly his. I read, and laughed, as I imagined the pleasure he must have had playing with words. He wrote about himself in the third person (*this made him laugh*, I am certain); I read a short note:

> Professor Yossef Hochberg, once a serious scientist, now looks down at his colleagues. *They* have no idea they are doing nothing but playing with *kaka*. Well, let them go on. Professor Hochberg has more important things to do that none of these lower minds [*mochot nemokhim*] could possibly understand.

I read on and thought to myself, *He wasn't just "mad."* He never stopped being quirky, mischievous, funny, and witty. Then, as I continued to shuffle through more papers, I found a text that made me laugh out loud. It also made me realize how much I loved this madman.

The text I found is titled "A Diet Poem" and is dated 2005. My dad uses elevated pious Hebrew to plead with God for divine intervention "to help him lose weight." The poem is written in rhymes, and I realize how difficult it would be for me to translate his brilliant, funny, and multilayered poem, which plays with different registers of Hebrew (high, low, biblical, modern), into English. I end up spending hours and hours laboring on the translation. A tough task, especially for a secular "bad Jew" like me, since it involves being able to capture the nuances of the archaic Hebrew while maintaining the meter and rhyme. I do my best to capture the humor and the craft:

> Ana Eli, Ana Eli, Ase Oti Kli le-shlichotkha
>
> Kli raze ve-shriri,
> lo shamen ve-chaziri
>
> La'asot ke-retsoncha be-lev shaelem,
> le-hargish tov ve lo ashem
>
> Bemakom sh'bo okhlim im chaverim,
> asena sh'ezkor, sh'hem razim
>
> Vekesh hem nehenim me-kinuchim,
> asena sh'ezkor et ha-tchorim

> [O my lord, O my lord, make me a vessel for your service
> A vessel, muscular and lean,
> not fat and unclean
>
> To follow your ways fully,
> feeling good, not unruly
>
> When among friends, please
> help me remember that they,
> unlike me, are slender
>
> And, when they enjoy their
> sweet course
> make me remember my
> hemorrhoid curse.]

Hemorrhoids. Yes. It appears that the one other main interest for my father, aside from God, messianism, Judaism, and his war against Christian science, was hemorrhoids. I find numerous notes about how much he suffered from them. But it wasn't just hemorrhoids that preoccupied him. His writings are equally invested (obsessed, really) with shit or, rather, with the act of shitting. I wish I could ignore these texts. I tried to. I'd avoided writing about his shit for five years, but alas, I can no longer do so. Shit is all over his archive, and I, his dutiful archivist, must keep a record. It would be disingenuous to clean up his archive. I have no choice; shit is everywhere.

Shit Matters

Why? I asked myself. *Why these endless musings on shit and shitting?* My discomfort was mounting. Most of his shit writings are centered on his "bad shitting." How could he think of himself as the promised Messiah *and* as such a shitty shitter?

Without the buffer of biblical quotes and the elevated poetic Hebrew register, his writing feels primal, vulgar, and bleeding. It moans and spews. I feel ashamed. For him, but also for me, for reading, translating, and rewriting it. Mostly I am appalled and embarrassed by how tantalized I feel despite my repulsion.

> I sit on the toilet for an hour, trying to stick the hemorrhoid back inside with my finger. It keeps coming out. I spit on my hand. This should help lubricate my anus. I hope this will keep the hemorrhoid inside.

Why on earth did he write this? Clearly, he didn't intend for anyone to read this, let alone his daughter. Yet, he wrote this, and similar notes, and kept them all. I try to shake off the image of my father sitting on the toilet engaging with his hemorrhoids, but it is already there, imprinted on my mind. And now I am passing it on to my readers.

I suspect any good editor would advise me to take these out, surely. These writings are good for nothing. But I can't. Not only because they are part of his archive, but also because in reading them, somehow I've always known that shit was central to my father. He often talked about shit and, later in life, smelled like shit.

He lived the last two decades of his life without a functioning digestive system and, after several failed operations, had a colostomy bag. Secured with layers of medical gauze and tape, hidden away behind big T-shirts and sweaters, it was supposed to be sealed, but it often leaked, which made him smell terrible. Miriam did her best to help him clean it up, but he always smelled like shit.

To clean up my dad's shit writings would be to violate my memories; but worse, it would be a deliberate act to hide parts of him to make him appear more dignified. Something about the idea of this purification makes me feel resentment. I refuse to hide his shit, and mine. It would make this whole experience of writing between bodies sanitized, and that is not the point. His body speaks of shit. I shall write shit with him.

I read on. Another note is titled: "How to Clean Ass." The title is highlighted with a yellow highlighter and three underlines. Clearly, this was an important matter for him. I read the text and alternated between shame, disgust, laughter, and crying. I rethink my decision: *Can I actually expose him like this? Should I really share such shitty writings?* I feel embarrassed to do so, not for him but for myself.

I show Keri the note and ask for her opinion. Her facial expression is one of repulsion. "Just leave these things out of the book," she says. "So gross. It's disrespectful of your dad, and no one needs to read this. No one *wants* to read this." I understand her position. She is likely right about it. Still, I can't keep them out. These writings are very much a part of him. It is precisely a matter of respect. He had nothing to hide. I have nothing to hide. I cannot hide him. Do not want to hide on his behalf.

These texts belong here, along with his musings on science, the Messiah, redemption, Judaism, world justice, and statistics. These texts are part of his body, and they are, if indirectly, also part of mine. Shitting doesn't come easily to me; I've suffered from chronic constipation since childhood. Shitting freaks me out. Uncomfortable and undignified as this makes me feel to share this, I must recognize that shit is part of my familial heritage. No less than my fear of annihilation.

I swallow my pride and make a firm decision to include these texts, wretched and revolting as they may be. Our bodies are connected across time and place. Shit is part of the glue. Writing between bodies.

1999

"How to Clean Ass—a Guide:"

1. Different people have different methods.

2. I, for one, take this matter seriously. First, I use lots of toilet paper and apply pressure on the hemorrhoids, pushing them inside. Second, I clean around the surrounding area. Third, I finalize with a gentle polish. And if necessary, I spit on the paper and lubricate the area.

3. Based on a survey I conducted for years in public restrooms, I conclude that most people wipe quickly, barely even thirty seconds, and hurry out. Clearly, they don't clean well.

4. The Talmud tells us about a group of yeshiva students who followed their rabbi to study how to clean ass. He told them *gam zo Torah* [This too is Torah and a lesson]. And, as with any Torah and lesson, knowledge requires practice. But the question remains: How do we practice ass cleaning?

5. What people do not know when they hurry up is that, like the yeshiva students, it is not enough to follow a lesson. Without practice, no learning is complete. Most people think they know how to wipe off their shit, but they're not following the Torah. They do not practice enough shit cleaning and fail to wipe properly.

6. So, *ma-hi ha-Torah*? [So, what is the lesson?] I follow the advice of the great rabbi and put it in my words: "After careful wiping, apply saliva and take time. Push the hemorrhoids. Then, follow with one final wipe. Rinse with water and make sure there is no shit left behind."

I could hardly believe it as I read it. Even when he writes about shit and ass cleaning, he makes references to the Talmud and rabbis, imaginary as those are likely to be. Only he could have possibly used such pious language to describe shit cleaning as a matter of rabbinic learning and Torah lessons. His inner worlds were one: abject and divine; shit and Torah. All are part of a single universe. A wild cosmos my father inhabited.

Soon enough, I find another shit text. This one is significantly more painful for me to read. It is personal and speaks of his terrible sense of inferiority in a way I hadn't found in any of his other writings. The text is titled "What? How? And When: Important Life Lessons." I read and my heart sank.

> I learned several important things very late in life. I learned how to have sex at age forty. And a decade later, when I turned fifty, I learned how to wipe my ass properly. My parents taught me some useful things about life, but only things that benefited them, like how I should behave in public or study to become a good student. They failed to teach me the most important things: how to have sex and how to clean my ass.
>
> I think there should be a protocol to ensure that every child gets to learn these two things, because without these two lessons (sex and ass cleaning), no one is ready for life. Any kid who has been brought up properly and was taught how to wipe his ass well has an advantage over others. They recognize when shitting is over, when to stop pushing, and when and how to clean. Those kids, when they grow up, never get hemorrhoids. They do not suffer, because they always know when to stop. People like this always fare better in life than someone like me. My parents failed to teach me these basic, important lessons, and without this knowledge I never really had a chance to thrive. No one can move forward in life without knowing when to stop pushing and without recognizing when shitting is over [matay ha-chirbon hegi'a le-siyumo].

I read his distressing note and cannot help but think how bitterly ironic and cruel it is that this man, who was so preoccupied with matters of ass cleaning and proper shitting, ended up unable to shit at all, wearing a colostomy around his middle, and smelling like shit constantly. How terribly tragic for him. And how humiliating it must have been for him to have to literally wear his internal sense of inadequacy out in public, even if it was hidden under his sweater.

I was just about to seal the "shit folder" and place it in back in the drawer, happy to move away from all shit matters, when I found another delightful and overtly outlandish text entitled "The Fart of Jericho, or The Divine Fart." This one is lighter and more fun to read as it brings together his fascination with the anus with his theological musings in a clearly humorous way. He wrote in numbered lines:

1. The event took place upon the entry of the Israelites to the Promised Land, 3,270 years ago.

2. God looked down on Jericho and realized that he was right to promise this land to the children of Abraham, because the Canaanite-ancestor was no better than shit; it was and smelled like ass shit.

3. God also realized that he was faced with a great opportunity to finally release a profound, joyful, divine fart, of the very same kind he has released only once before, at Mount Sinai.

4. He realized that the last godly fart he released sounded and looked like an atomic bomb. And that *beni yisrael* trust in him and his farts of redemption.

5. He encouraged the children of Israel, who did not fear his mighty fart, to march toward the walls of Jericho and circle the walls seven times while he went on farting.

6. His final divine fart was colossal and sounded and smelled like a real stinky atomic bomb *p'tsa'tsat sirachon atomit*. Which is why the city is called "Jericho." The name comes from the Hebrew word *Ya-ri-cho*, which means "and they shall smell." For whoever was there smelled the divine fart that made the city walls fall.

Unlike his painful shit texts, this one represents my father's toilet humor. I cannot help but think of Freud writing about the anal stage. My dad seemed to have gotten stuck there. He even wrote national fables from this place. Anus, ass, fart, shit.

His words oscillate between totally crazy and brilliantly hilarious. Reading him makes me laugh and cry in turns. This man, who by age forty-five decided he was the Messiah, writes:

> I am losing interest in my academic work. I have no more belief in science and no more respect for numbers. I only believe in my own Holy Trinity: "Miriam, Farts, and Shit."

This Holy Trinity, my dad goes on writing,

> is the foundation for my new self and new position as the Messiah. I shall shit and fart out the remains of the delusion of science within me, the curse brought upon us all by Christianity.

I am sad to not be included in his new world order and to not be part of his holy trinity. But I am comforted by the thought that somehow, despite all the suffering and depression he endured, he managed to create an eternal world that made sense to him. Even if it mixed his messianic grandeur with his utter preoccupation with shit. One thing remained certain for him, or at least so it seems: Christianity was the cause of all hell—science, psychiatry, rationalism, and philosophy. Jews were meant to believe in no one but the one and only: he who farts the loudest, Elohim.

If only he knew when to stop, I reflect to myself, sadly. But he couldn't. My dad, who truly believed he was the Messiah, was nevertheless filled with darkness and pain, pulled down by a haunting sense of inferiority. He felt robbed: "A child's success depends on being taught when shitting is actually over, and when to stop pushing." He was not loved enough, not taught well enough, had not been given the tools to succeed. How could he possibly succeed when he didn't even learn "when to stop pushing"?

If only he knew when to stop. Instead, his body, afflicted with self-harm, bruised, scarred, cut, and bloated, became the battlefield where his two sides—his abjection and his grander, messianic drive—kept fighting each other. Until, eventually, his ego shattered, his body collapsed, and he came to a halt.

2024

New York

My Siddur

June 2024. By now I'd reread all of my father's writings numerous times and was certain there was nothing I had left unturned. A friend who'd never visited my home study before wandered in, looked at my bookshelf, and pulled out a thick, brown leather hardcover book. "Is this Hebrew?" she asked.

I don't think I'd ever noticed this book until that moment. A siddur (Hebrew daily prayers). I was utterly surprised when she found it, buried among my queer, feminist, postcolonial, and critical race studies books. Once she left,

I opened the book and found, to my great surprise, a long, handwritten dedication from my dad on the first page. *Of course. Who else would give me a siddur?* I thought and went on reading.

He congratulates me for my twenty-eighth birthday using the Hebrew letters כ"ח. Then he adds a blessing, "May God give you *Strength*," which in Hebrew is written almost the same, כח. I smile as I read it, imagining that this cleverness must have given him great satisfaction. If there was something his writings taught me, it was that he absolutely *loved* playing with his mastery of Hebrew, using rare linguistic coins, rhyming, and clashing humorlessly between the different registers of language. His Hebrew was especially rich thanks to his yeshiva upbringing. He mastered biblical Hebrew but also knew all the rabbinical phrases and expressions, most of which were in Aramaic. His writing was dense, as his Hebrew was much richer than that of most secular Israelis, myself included.

I went on reading, surprised that even while reading his moving words, I had no memory of ever reading this before. I suppose when one is young one pays less attention. You don't think about the fragility of life. I was a graduate student when he gave me this siddur. I was preoccupied with my studies and my social life. I must have read it and forgotten all about it. I didn't foresee the possibility of losing him.

I am surprised that in his dedication to me he chose to share the painful biblical story of Issac's bonding. A strange (daring but also perverse) choice for a father to share with his only child. "Le-beetee, asher ahavti" (My daughter, whom I've loved), he writes, using Abraham's words to Isaac, only changing *son* to *daughter*. Then he continues:

> Every morning when I read the story of the *Akedha* [Bonding], one of the pillars of Judaism, I feel mortified. I try to understand Abraham. How could he? How was he willing to sacrifice his own son to prove his dedication to God? How was he able to go through the motions: tying his son to the altar, then lifting the knife to cut his throat. It is truly unthinkable! And every time I read this, I feel relieved that times have changed. That God no longer needs to put his followers though such terrible tests. By now, his doctrine, monotheism, and revelation are secured. He has created a people: We, the people of Israel, are committed to the Torah and the mitzvot. He no longer needs proof of that. We ought to be grateful to Abraham and the following generations of our pious fathers. Thanks to them, we no longer need to go through such hard ordeals.
>
> My Daughter, whom I love: I give you this book of Jewish prayers with the hope that you will read and remember. That you will develop a strong love for your

roots, for your people, for your fathers, and for your language (Hebrew), and for Judaism, which doesn't tell the difference of times: *What was then is now.*

You, my child, whom I have loved; You my child who I love now. This book belongs to you. These prayers belong to you. Then and Now.

Love you,
ABBA

Moved by his words, I make a promise to myself (whom I hardly trust) that "I will make this book and these prayers mine." Despite feeling quite reluctant, I open the siddur and read, if only for a short while.

His Voice, Mine

The other day I was walking with a close friend in Riverside Park, making our way from my apartment at 116th, downtown toward west Sixty-Sixth Street, when she surprised me with an unexpected question, "Where is your voice coming from? Is it your dad's?" I'd never thought about my voice in relation to anyone, but my friend continued: "Because I know your mother's voice and it certainly isn't hers."

Do children inherit their parents' voices? I'd found clear marks and traces of my father in my toes, which are very similar to his, in the curve at the top of my spine, in the strength of my hands, in my short fingers, high forehead, thick eyebrows, meaty lips, and in my smile, but I'd never considered my voice in relation to his. Never. Even when I lost my body in his words. During this whole time of archiving, reading every word he wrote, copying and translating him as I tried to create my own language, I was only always thinking about text: words, paper, the materiality of the writing, the marks of his pen. Text but never sound. My friend's question intrigued me: *Do I even remember his voice?*

I have so many photos of him. I collected them after his death. Photos of him as a baby, a toddler, a young child, a teen, a young man, a young father, a husband, a professor, an older father, an older man, a sick man, a man swollen and puffed up with cortisone. When I close my eyes, I can see lots of images floating before me like a silent film. I can imagine him, clear and visible, in various positions and formations, smiling, concentrating, young, old, child, adult.

I have all his texts—I know his writing so well, and I know the difference between his youthful writing and his later, shakier writing. I know his poetic voice and his prosaic voice. I have images and words. *But the sound of his voice? Can I remember his actual voice? Can I hear his voice in mine?*

We used to sing together. Our voices merging. He was a great singer; I always loved listening to him sing. I remember the settings, the songs, the joy of "going Hasidic" together: *ko amar ko amar ha-shem* . . . we sang together at the top of our voices. But when I try to remember the sound of his voice, all I get is an image. I am unable to generate a sound memory.

Photographs can conjure the sense of the dead looking back at us. I stare into his eyes. I can even see him as a child, before I was born. His writings too speak to me, but voicelessly. I wish I had a tape recording. I call Haim, hoping his voice would remind me of his, but my uncle's voice and tone are completely different. My father's voice was deeper. Much deeper. How I wish I could hear it again.

My writing cannot revive my father's voice. Like other texts, it remains silent. But strangely, during these years of writing about him, *about* and *with* his writings, I never felt we were writing. No. I felt we were singing. *I was a kid and he was my dad, and we're singing Hasidic songs together.* The feeling was always fleeting. It came and left, always leaving me with an image of his sad eyes. Maybe because he, like me, knew this was just a fantasy. Writing cannot bring back the past. We always ended up apart.

I sing softly now, alone. No audience. My voice is deep and low. I like it. I listen to myself. My voice feels familiar. More than my skin, or my writing, or my face, I recognize my voice as mine. It hold within it *our* voices together, his and mine, daughter and father singing together. *Ashira La-shem be-chayai, yai, yai, azamra le-elokie be'odi.* We sing together in Hebrew, and I realize that this is as close as I can possibly get to hearing his voice again.

Let Me Out!

A few days before he died, my father got up from his hospital bed in the ICU, feverish and delusional. It was not the typical "terminal lucidity" people associate with the sudden increased energy and mental clarity many patients experience close to death. His abrupt energy was frantic, hallucinatory, and stormy. He woke screaming at everyone to let him out: "World redemption depends on me! LET ME OUT NOW." He was the Messiah in captivity. Soon after that, he was connected to life support, unconscious. Deflated and lifeless. He never woke up or spoke again. "Let me out" were his final words.

After spending so many years reading him, archiving his words, preserving his papers, translating his texts, writing with and about him, I was about to let his words out to the world. I hope this will "let him out" and at least partly fulfill his last request.

I wanted to let him out of the inner, closed walls of my mind and let his words out of the hidden box in which he kept them for decades. Letting him out is sharing his brilliance, his humor, his blazing mind, his ambition, his mischievousness, his parental love, his imagination, his playfulness. But also his torment, his depression, his mania, his madness, violence, compulsion, abjecthood, and delusional messianism.

All of these have left significant imprints on me and made me who I am and who I may still become. In some ways, I am his living, organic archive. I am the daughter of an unrecognized Messiah; one among many self-claimed false Messiahs in Judaism. Indeed, my dad finds himself in the good company of Yeshua of Nazareth, Shimon Bar Kokhva, Moshe of Crete, Abu-Isa, Moshe al-Da'ri, David Alroy (Menahem ben Solomon), Shlomo Molcho, Asher Kay, Shabbtai Zevi, Jacob Josef Frank, Menachem Mendel Schneerson, and others.

All Messiahs are false, but some enjoy fame, while others are forgotten. My father was a lonely and tragic Messiah. Unlike his fellow self-proclaimed Messiahs, he had no followers. None but his devoted wife. He brought on no wars, created no sects, made no conversions, led no rebellion.

As a statistician, he was a key figure in the subfield of false discovery (revelations) rate. As a Messiah, he focused attention on divine revelations. For the first, he earned worldwide recognition; for the latter, he was mocked and ignored. I wish I had given him more of the recognition he craved so badly when he was alive. But I didn't. I insisted on making it clear to him that I was not a believer: not in his messianism or in his God. I regret this. I should have pretended I did, just like I had when I was a kid and pretended to believe all the fables he told me about his magnificent gifts, powers, and capacities. *It wouldn't have caused any harm*, I reflect remorsefully, *and it would have made him happy.*

August 2024

Rebordões

Impossible Ending

I flew out to Portugal for three weeks with a clear goal in mind: finish the book. It had been more than six years. I had revisited and rewritten, already compiling four different drafts, each with a different structure. I'd had endless imaginary conversations with my dad in my head. I'd read every text of his at least twice. I looked through all the family albums. I met and spoke to all the living relatives. It was time to let go. I knew it. I felt it. My writing was gradually moving from a place of compassion to a place of compulsion. But the hardest task was still ahead of me: ending. Endings are hard. Much harder for me than beginnings. In this case, the task felt particularly daunting. Writing about/with him for so long had blurred the borders between us. Between our bodies, psyches, memories, voices, even sexualities. *Whose words should I end with? His? Mine?*

My looped chain of thoughts was brought to a standstill unexpectedly when a name from the past appeared in my inbox: Yoav Benjamini. My father's colleague and collaborator. We last talked in 2022, when I asked him, over Zoom, to tell me about his experience working with my dad. Why was he writing me? Why now? Something about seeing his name in my inbox terrified me (what could he possibly be writing me about?!), and for a split second, a crazy thought passed through my mind: *He is writing to let me know my dad died.* I shook myself, came back to my senses, then opened and read his email:

Gil Shalom,

Hope all is well with you and your family.

The Rousseeuw Prize was awarded to me and my former students Ruth Heller and Dani Yekutieli for our research on the false discovery rate. The prestigious award is supposed to be equivalent to the Nobel Prize, which is known not to be awarded in fields such as mathematics or statistics, and is awarded by the King of Belgium.

I am attaching the photo from the website and the link where there is further detail about our contribution (in a not-too-statistical language) and the award, where you will also read about the explicit mention of your dad's important contribution.

Happy to send you this recognition of the achievements in our work that began in cooperation with Yossi. Too bad he isn't here with us.

Best regards,
Yoav

It was kind of Yoav to send the note. Still, "too bad he isn't here with us" failed to resonate with the intensity of emotions I felt upon reading it: a mix of pride, frustration, and deep sorrowfulness. I felt sick, as if someone had just punched me in the gut.

The official announcement included the line: "Yosef Hochberg also deserved much recognition, but unfortunately he is no longer with us."[40] Like Yoav's note and the newspaper article that was published later in the day, it paid tribute to my father and recognized his important contribution. I tried very hard to feel pride on his behalf. To celebrate him. But I couldn't fight the feeling that crept in: The belatedness of the recognition sharpened my view of him as a tragic figure.

His great contributions to "modern statistics" and "scientific research more broadly" arrived too late; *at least eleven years too late.* He "was no longer with us." He missed his own party. New guests, younger students, arrived and benefited from the fruit of his labor.

This bitterness filled me with shame. I tried to fight it by sharing the news with Eli and Omri, with friends, and with my mom, who felt proud for him and told me: "I still remember how, when we first met, and we were both first-year college students, he said to me: 'I'm a genius and I'm going to change the face of statistics.' I guess he did." But the more I labored to feel pride and celebrate his recognition, the more acute my grief became.

The news reopened my wound. I was ready to finally move on when the prize (or was it the flat words, announcing it was "too bad" that "he was gone"?) caused my pain to resurface. It reminded me that mourning is uncontainable. One cannot control it or decide when it is done. Mourning doesn't follow linear time or structure. This acute feeling of distress came with some relief. I no longer had to even *try* to create a false narrative of progress: from mourning to recovery.

I wonder how he would have reacted to the news if he were "still with us today." Would he have felt proud? Would he have celebrated his past achievements? Or would he have dismissed it all as "false discoveries"—part of what he had come to refer to as "Christian lies"? I am not sure. My father has not been with us for quite some time now. Not just since his death in 2013, but at least twenty years beforehand.

The years building up to his first major breakdown in 1991 were clouded with professional doubt. I learned about this mostly from Yoav, in 2022, when he told me about my father's original ideas and how, back in the late 1980s and early 1990s, no one thought his new ideas made any sense: "He faced a lot of resistance, but that is the case with all scientific revelations."

Back in the 1990s, I was young and had no idea my father was going through a difficult time with his academic career. How much it contributed to his breakdown is hard to tell, but reading the award announcement I become aware, for the first time, of the profound rejection he must have experienced back then. And knowing well, by now, how much he was unable to tolerate rejection, I feel certain this must have played a major role in what spiraled into his first acute depressive episode. One from which he never fully came back.

The announcement highlights the romantic narrative of a great scientific breakthrough, which starts with repeated rejections but leads to a victorious success:

> The international and independent jury, appointed by the King Baudouin Foundation, has selected the pioneering work on the False Discovery Rate (FDR) as the recipient of the biennial Rousseeuw Prize for Statistics 2024.... The 1995 paper by Benjamini and Hochberg introduced FDR, providing a framework for further expansion and publications.... In 1995, Benjamini and Hochberg published a mathematical formulation of the False Discovery Rate (FDR) criterion, as the expected ratio of false discoveries to the total number of discoveries.... At first glance, their suggestion seems impossible because we do not know beforehand how many false discoveries there are, but they found a way to do it.... Their paper faced much resistance because it differed so greatly from previous methods, resulting in five years passing and three journals being approached before it finally appeared in 1995. To date, the paper by Benjamini and Hochberg has been cited over 100,000 times, a record number.[41]

"Their paper faced much resistance because it differed so greatly from previous methods, resulting in five years passing and three journals being approached before it finally appeared in 1995." Those five years were years of acute torment for my father. Coupled with what was a very late-in-life diagnosis of bipolar disorder, these repeated rejections sent him off, first to the heights of manic delusions and then, soon after, to the bottom of morbid depression. From then on, while he would teach and even publish, he was never the same man. At best, he became a half-alive half-man. The tragic figure I still mourn.

By the time the essay came out in 1995, and was since "cited over 100,000 times, a record number," he was long gone and unable to enjoy the success.[42] Lost to depression, various illnesses of body and mind, and eventually dead, my dad took no part in this glory. *Can I?*

I tried hard to fight my mounting sense of bitterness. It was uncalled for and unproductive. No one was responsible for his suffering, for his illnesses, for his death. I decided to focus instead on being proud on his behalf. But the nagging sense of the bad timing refused to go. There was something so cruel and tragic about the belatedness of the recognition. *Why now, why so late . . . eleven years late?*

Then, just as I was about to sink back into my well of resentment, it hit me: I've been thinking about all of this in the wrong way. And surely not in *his way*. I got the whole timing wrong! *Too late?* Totally wrong! That is surely not how he would have seen this. And what was the whole point of the lesson he gave me about "Jewish time"? Judaism, he writes, "doesn't tell the difference of times: what was then is now." Of course. My father, my cowriter, would have had a totally different spin on this latest chain of events.

During the last two decades of his life, my father, once a dedicated statistician committed to narrowing the gap of scientific false discoveries, changed his worldview and began to read all events in terms of omens and divine revelations. *What would he say?*

I'd been having imaginary conversations with him for the past six years, while awake and in my dreams. We had been writing together, sharing secrets, laughing, and crying. Catching up on everything we'd missed. It made perfect sense for me to close my eyes, turn my attention inward, and ask him: "What do you think?"

"*Yaldati*," he begins, "don't you see what this is all about?"

"What is it all about?" I ask.

"This is a sign, Gilly. A message *for you*."

"What message? For me? From whom? What about?"

"A sign of divine intervention, which is always on time."

"What intervention? You are long gone..."

"Forget about the prize and the recognition! Those don't matter. *Inyanai dyuma*. The only thing that matters is *geula* [redemption]."

"What redemption? What are you talking about?"

"Your own, *yaldati*, your own."

"Mine? What redemption do I need?"

"Well," he answers measuredly, "for one, the news came out just in time for you to include it in the book about me. Second, you must be able to see that none of this is a coincidence... Even you, cynical and secular as you may be, must see... News like this delivered *just in time*... perfect timing, *yaldati*, perfect timing. Even you must admit, *nes nisi* [a miracle of miracles]."

"I'm not sure I follow," I reply, waiting for his enthusiastic response that indeed doesn't fail to follow: "One day, *yaldati*, one day you too will be able and willing to see. *He* sent you the news. It is all part of His mighty plan. He saw your struggle and your pain. Your fear that if you stop writing I will disappear. He sent you the news, just in time. *Perfect timing!* He wanted you to realize that I am already remembered by the entire world! My name is already on the books; my essay has been cited more than 100,000 times, record-breaking. He wanted you to know that you can stop now. I am remembered. You can rest now. And one day, my daughter, one day you too will see all this and believe."

I dream up this conversation. I write his words and read them, too. *He, me, us.* "What was then is now." Why think linearly? With that I agree.

I cannot (and will not) convince myself that any of this is true (divine intervention? miracle? sign?), no. But I don't need to. I have him to do that for me. He holds that narrative. *What was then is now.* His words are already mine. The mere ability to articulate this celestial narrative and put it in words is sufficient. *I write his words and read them too.*

It helps elevate me from my earlier state of anguish. I adopt a (his) calm outlook instead:

"Everything is in place.

"Everything is on time.

"What was then is now.

"His words, mine."

I am the daughter of a once-great statistician who later in life rejected science and became instead a self-appointed Messiah. A man who spoke in tongues and believed in miracles. A man who fell victim to his mental illness and whose sick body failed him, too. But this is not a story of his fall from grace. He would have objected to such a narrative fiercely. "What was then is now." *Fall* and *grace* belong to a very different cosmology. A Christian Weltanschauung, which he rejected vehemently.

I shall, like his fellow scientists, remember him as a man who greatly contributed to modern statistics, whose essay's citation still breaks records. But I will also remember him as a man who believed he was communicating with God, sending and receiving coded messages, standing in trials, and hoping to prove himself worthy of becoming the real Messiah.

He always knew my skepticism and doubts. He always knew I was not a believer: not in his messianism or in his God. It hurt him, greatly, I've learned from reading him. But with time, and through our shared writings, we have reached an agreement: I don't have to believe in order to accept. I don't have to believe in order to celebrate. *What was then is now.* I pour myself a glass of white wine, look at his photo placed on my desk, lift my glass up high, smile at him, and say:

"To Yossi!"

"To my father!"

"My father, the Messiah!"

I sip, close my eyes, and hear him say, "Le-Yossi."

His voice, mine.

"His voice, mine." Chapel Hill, North Carolina, 1972.

Acknowledgments

This book is a work of love and pain. Many voices fueled it and saved me from the loneliness of writing.

Between 2019 and 2021, I participated in a few creative writing workshops in New York. Megan Barry, Mike Day, Nicole Desiree, Gisela Mandl, Olivia McGill, Stacy Pershall, Jil Picariello, Danna Walker, and Victoria Yoffie were the first readers of early iterations of this project. I thank them deeply for their insightful feedback and for sharing their own writings with me. They have provided me with inspiration and a sense of community.

A heartfelt gratitude is extended to Alysia Abbott and Ruth Novaczek, each of whom read and commented extensively on earlier versions of this manuscript. Their careful engagement and astute editorial suggestions helped me move forward.

My dear friend Tamar Assal read and commented on several drafts of this book over the long years. I thank her for so many conversations. Her attentiveness, love, and ongoing encouragement have served as my rock.

A huge gratitude goes to Courtney Berger, whose belief in this project and strong support for it have kept me going at times of doubt. I am immensely thankful for her editorial skills and friendship.

Other friends and colleagues have discussed various aspects of the work with me over the years. I thank Sadia Abbas, Noa Ben Ahser, Yael Bartana, Mel Y. Chen, Sarah Cole, Mikhal Dekel, Mamdou Diouf, Galit Eilat, Jack Halberstam, Naomi Kanyuk, Julee S. Peters, and Nataly Shahaf for many enticing conversations about messianism, memoir writing, memory, and queer survival. It is always reassuring to know one is not alone in one's esoteric pursuits.

A mighty grand gratitude is reserved for Ayelet Ben Yishai. Many pages of this book have been written and rewritten in her company over summers spent together in our dual writing retreats. I cannot imagine being able to have done it otherwise. I thank her for her fierce intellectual engagement, long friendship, and, no less important, the numerous unforgettable dinners she has cooked for the two of us over the years.

For copyediting I thank Erin Ivy and Colleen Jankovic. Each worked on different versions of this manuscript. Colleen has always been much more than an editor for me. I thank her for her passionate engagement with my writing, her humor, and her friendship. This is the third book we have worked on together. I wouldn't have it any other way.

Laura Jaramillo, Lisa Lawley, Ziggy Snow, and the entire production team at Duke University Press deserve great appreciation for their hard work and support. As do my two readers: Laura Levitt, who "came out" to me as one of the two anonymous readers, and Reader #2. Both provided me with generously detailed reviews and brilliant constructive feedback, which have surely made this book better.

Immense gratitude is reserved for my father's family: to my uncle Haim Hochberg, for passing on family stories and for his support throughout this long process, and for my father's cousins Leah Katz, Batia Londin, Yossi Gal, and Benny Glikman, for opening their hearts and homes to me and sharing anecdotes and images of my father. I am also indebted to my mother, Ruth Ramot, who shared so many memories with me—some beautiful, some painful. She has been a close interlocutor throughout this long journey, and I know it has not always been an easy ride. I thank my brothers, Daniel Tsur and Itamar Tsur, for their supporting love and hugs.

A very special thanks goes to professors Yoav Benjamini and Ajit C. Tamhane for the time they each spent talking to me about my father's academic career and for the patience they've shown in trying to make me understand his contributions to statistics. Their generosity and kindness far exceeded my limited ability to grasp the modern science of collecting and analyzing data.

I wish to also thank Kathleen McIntyre for encouraging me to delve deep into the past. Knowing that she will always be there to help me come back made it possible.

I met Laurie Lathem during the final year of this long writing process. I am indebted to her for so many evocative conversations about writing and reading. These have greatly fueled my imagination and filled me with joy.

I am full of deep appreciation to Keri Kanetsky for reading and rereading so many sections of this book over and over again, even when I refused to take certain parts out despite her protest. She continues to be my confidant and harshest loving critic. I'm grateful for that and so much more.

My kids, Eli Kanetsky and Omri Kanetsky: I thank you for listening to all my stories about grandfather Yossi and great-grandparents Hirschel and Tsipe. Your laughter and enthusiasm encouraged me to write these all down.

Last but not least: Thank you, Dad, for everything. I hope you enjoy the read.

Notes

1. Benjamin, "Theses on the Philosophy of History," 259.
2. Following the 1948 war, Jerusalem was divided: The western part came under Israel's rule and East Jerusalem under Jordan's control. After the 1967 war, Israel conquered East Jerusalem and the West Bank and declared the whole of the city—both western and eastern parts—as its capital. The international community has generally never recognized Israeli sovereignty over East Jerusalem. In 2017, President Donald Trump announced US recognition of Jerusalem as Israel's capital and moved the US embassy from Tel Aviv to Jerusalem. Only a handful of nations in the United Nations voted along with the United States and similarly moved their embassies to Jerusalem—among them: Guatemala, Honduras, and Kosovo. In July 2024, the United Nations' top court (the International Court of Justice) declared that Israel's presence in East Jerusalem is illegal. Also see Hochberg, "This City That Isn't One."
3. *Sepsis* derives from the Greek word σήψη meaning "decay" or "decomposition." See Vincent, "Evolution of the Concept of Sepsis"; Funk, Parrillo, and Kumar, "Sepsis and Septic Shock."
4. Erlichman, *Odes to Lithium*, 41. The source passage reads: "Yellow, slutty tree, oh cerebellum, oh lithium, do your job."
5. Lowe, "Lithium, Love and Losing."
6. Jamison, *An Unquiet Mind*, 258.
7. Moses ben Maimon (1135–1204—commonly known as Maimonides and also referred to by the Hebrew *Rambam* (רמב״ם), the acronym for Rabbi Moses ben Maimon, was a rabbi and philosopher who remains the best-known Jewish writer and thinker of the Middle Ages, if not of all time.
8. Grand Rabbi Gershon Chanoch Henech Leiner of Radzyn (1839–December 15, 1890) was known for his research on the restoration of the original blue color of the

tzitzit, concluding that it was extracted from the secretion of a certain snail or catfish. He is therefore also known by the nickname Ba'al ha-tekhelet (Master of the Blue).

9. Tzitzit are the specially knotted ritual fringes, or tassels, attached to the four corners of the tallit (prayer shawl). There is a long debate among different groups of Hasidim about the color of the tzitzit and whether it should or should not be dyed in blue.

10. Rabbi Solomon ben Isaac (1040–1105).

11. If this book had followed the five-stage story arc, this chapter no doubt would have been the climax. (Gustav Freytag, a German novelist and playwright who closely analyzed ancient Greek writing along with William Shakespeare's five-act plays, outlined the five-stage story arc in his book *Die Technik des Dramas*.)

12. Said, "Reflections on Exile." See also Said, *Out of Place*.

13. Hebron (Al-Khalil in Arabic) is the largest city in the West Bank and the only city in the Occupied Palestinian Territory apart from Jerusalem with illegal settlements inside the city. In 1997, the Hebron Protocol placed the majority of the city, to be known as H1, under the control of the Palestinian Authority and the remaining 20 percent, named H2, under direct Israeli control. In the H2 section, there are approximately eight hundred Jews and forty thousand Palestinians living in strict separation. The Israeli army operates a prolific network of checkpoints and watchtowers throughout the city and enforces severe restrictions of movement on the Palestinian population, allegedly to secure the safety of the Jewish settlers.

14. Freud, "Mourning and Melancholia," 245.

15. Freud, "Mourning and Melancholia," 252.

16. Hochberg, *Visual Occupations*.

17. Freud, "Mourning and Melancholia," 248.

18. I am loosely alluding to Freud's *Beyond the Pleasure Principle*.

19. Established in the early 1970s, the London boys' choir Pirchei London (sometimes known as the London School of Jewish Song and the London Jewish Boys' Choir) performed Hasidic music around the world. My dad owned all their vinyl records.

20. *Free to Be . . . You and Me* was created and executive-produced by actress and author Marlo Thomas. A record album was first released in November 1972 (featuring Alan Alda, Rosey Grier, Cicely Tyson, Carol Channing, Michael Jackson, Roberta Flack, Shirley Jones, Jack Cassidy, and Diana Ross). An illustrated book and ABC television special, also created by Thomas, using poetry, songs, and sketches, followed two years later in March 1974. Thomas and Friends, *Free to Be . . . You and Me* (1972); Thomas and Friends, *Free to Be . . . You and Me* (1974); Davis, Steckler, and Wolf, *Free to Be . . . You and Me*.

21. The New Seekers, "Free to Be . . . You and Me," track no. 1 on Thomas and Friends, *Free to Be . . . You and Me* (1972).

22. Diana Ross, "When We Grow Up," track no. 3 on Thomas and Friends, *Free to Be . . . You and Me* (1972).

23. The New Seekers, "Free to Be . . . You and Me," track no. 1 on Thomas and Friends, *Free to Be . . . You and Me* (1972).

24. Klein, *Psycho-Analysis of Children*.

25. Winnicott, *Playing and Reality*, 53.

26. Freud, "'Child Is Being Beaten.'"

27. "It is surprising how often people who seek analytic treatment for hysteria or an obsessional neurosis confess to having indulged in the phantasy: 'A child is being beaten.' Very probably there are still more frequent instances of it among the far greater number of people who have not been obliged to come to analysis by manifest illness." Freud, "'Child Is Being Beaten,'" 179.

28. Steedman, *Dust*, 69; Derrida, "*Archive Fever*," 91.

29. Steedman, *Dust*, 164.

30. Barthes, *Camera Lucida*.

31. Klein, "Notes on Some Schizoid Mechanisms."

32. Miller, *Getting Personal*.

33. Miller, *Getting Personal*, 144.

34. Hampl, *I Could Tell You Stories*, 25.

35. Benjamini and Hochberg, "Controlling the False Discovery Rate," 292.

36. Bnei Akiva ("Children of Akiva") is the largest religious Zionist youth movement in the world, with members in forty-two countries. It was first established in Mandatory Palestine in 1929 and is currently the central Jewish Zionist youth movement in Israel. While originally considered centric, it has grown more right-wing in its ideology. For more on this, see Maltz, "Bnei Akiva Used to Fight Kahanism."

37. The State of Israel requires every Israeli citizen over the age of eighteen who is Jewish, Druze, or Circassian to serve in the army. Palestinian citizens of Israel, religious women, and certain yeshiva students are exempt. Compulsory military service is a minimum of thirty-two months for men and a minimum of twenty-four months for women.

38. Benjamin, "Theses on the Philosophy of History," 259.

39. The Jewish American Bund was a socialist party concerned with uniting other American labor parties and the Jewish Left globally.

40. Rousseeuw Prize for Statistics.

41. Rousseeuw Prize for Statistics.

42. Benjamini and Hochberg, "Controlling the False Discovery Rate."

Bibliography

Barthes, Roland. *Camera Lucida: Reflections on Photography*. Hill and Wang, 1981.
Benjamin, Walter. "Theses on the Philosophy of History." In *Illuminations: Essays and Reflections*. Edited by Hannah Arendt. Translated by Harry Zohn. Schocken Books, 1969.
Benjamini, Yoav, and Yosef Hochberg. "Controlling the False Discovery Rate: A Practical and Powerful Approach to Multiple Testing." *Journal of the Royal Statistical Society: Series B* 57, no. 1 (1995): 289–300.
Davis, Bill, Len Steckler, and Fred Wolf, dirs. *Free to Be . . . You and Me*. Aired March 11, 1974, on ABC.
Derrida, Jacques. *Archive Fever: A Freudian Impression*. Translated by Eric Prenowitz. University of Chicago Press, 1998.
Erlichman, Shira. *Odes to Lithium*. Alice James Books, 2019.
Freud, Sigmund. *Beyond the Pleasure Principle*. Liveright, 1961.
Freud, Sigmund. "'A Child Is Being Beaten': A Contribution to the Study of the Origin of Sexual Perversions." In *The Standard Edition of the Complete Psychological Works of Sigmund Freud*, vol. 17.
Freud, Sigmund. "Mourning and Melancholia." In *The Standard Edition of the Complete Psychological Works of Sigmund Freud*, vol. 14.
Freud, Sigmund. *The Standard Edition of the Complete Psychological Works of Sigmund Freud*. 24 vols. Edited by James Strachey. Hogarth, 1955. Originally published 1917.
Freytag, Gustav. *Die Technik des Dramas*. Salomon Hirzel, 1863.
Funk, Duane J., Joseph E. Parrillo, and Anand Kumar. "Sepsis and Septic Shock: A History." *Critical Care Clinics*, no. 25 (2009): 83–101.
Hampl, Patricia. *I Could Tell You Stories: Sojourns in the Land of Memory*. W. W. Norton, 1999.

Hochberg, Gil. "This City That Isn't One: Fragments on a Fragmented City." Contending Modernities, December 20, 2017. https://contendingmodernities.nd.edu/global-currents/fragmented-city/.

Hochberg, Gil Z. *Visual Occupations: Violence and Visibility in a Conflict Zone*. Duke University Press, 2015.

Hochberg, Yosef, and Ajit C. Tamhane. *Multiple Comparison Procedures*. Wiley, 1987.

Jamison, Kay Redfield. *An Unquiet Mind: A Memoir of Moods and Madness*. Vintage Books, 1996.

Klein, Melanie. "Notes on Some Schizoid Mechanisms." *International Journal of Psycho-analysis* 27 (1946): 99–110.

Klein, Melanie. *The Psycho-Analysis of Children*. Hogarth Press, 1932.

Lowe, Jaime. "Lithium, Love and Losing My Mind: Jaime Lowe on Her Life with Bipolar Disorder & Drugs to Manage It." Interview by Amy Goodman. *Democracy Now!*, December 28, 2017. https://www.democracynow.org/2017/12/28/lithium_love_and_losing_my_mind.

Lowe, Jaime. *Mental: Lithium, Love, and Losing My Mind*. Blue Rider Press, 2017.

Maltz, Judy. "Bnei Akiva Used to Fight Kahanism. Now the Youth Movement Has Embraced the Far Right." *Haaretz*, November 8, 2022. https://www.haaretz.com/israel-news/elections/2022-11-08/ty-article/.premium/this-youth-movement-once-fought-kahanism-now-it-provides-its-successor-with-lawmakers/00000184-52ff-de9c-a1c4-7fff7eb50000.

Miller, Nancy K. *Getting Personal: Feminist Occasions and Other Autobiographical Acts*. Routledge, 2014.

Rousseeuw Prize for Statistics. "The Rousseeuw Prize for Statistics 2024: False Discovery Rate and Methods to Control It." Accessed May 7, 2025. https://www.rousseeuwprize.org/2024.

Said, Edward W. *Out of Place: A Memoir*. Vintage, 2000.

Said, Edward W. "Reflections on Exile." *Granta*, September 1, 1984. https://granta.com/reflections-on-exile/.

Steedman, Carolyn. *Dust: The Archive and Cultural History*. Rutgers University Press, 2002.

Thomas, Marlo, and Friends. *Free to Be ... You and Me*. Produced by Carole Hart. Bell Records, November 1972.

Thomas, Marlo, and Friends. *Free to Be ... You and Me*. McGraw-Hill, 1974.

Vincent, Jean-Louis. "Evolution of the Concept of Sepsis." *Antibiotics* (Basel) 11, no. 11 (Nov. 9, 2022): 1581. doi: 10.3390/antibiotics11111581.

Winnicott, D. W. *Playing and Reality*. Routledge, 1971.

www.ingramcontent.com/pod-product-compliance
Lightning Source LLC
Chambersburg PA
CBHW020238170426
43202CB00008B/138